THE MINIMALIST BUDGET MINDSET

Learn how to eliminate compulsive spending
Learn ways to budget your money effectively and get out of debt
Learn ways to save and invest to achieve financial independence

Additionally, the information in the following pages is intended only for informational purposes and should thus be thought of as universal. As befitting its nature, it is presented without assurance regarding its prolonged validity or interim quality. Trademarks that are mentioned are done without written consent and can in no way be considered an endorsement from the trademark holder.

Table of Contents

Introduction

The Minimalist Budget Mindset is a guide to help you save money, spend less and live more efficiently with a minimalist lifestyle.

Most people approach budgeting with a deflated spirit and they see it as an impossible thing to achieve. They imagine that budgeting will only give them discomfort and strain. Sometimes even without making the effort, they think they are wholly incompatible with budgeting of any kind.

This book will give you a different approach to budgeting. It's truly unfortunate that the idea of living within your means should be experienced as such a deficit. It brings, after all, an abundance of benefits that most are unaware of. You'll soon see what we mean. This book will show you that when you live a minimalist lifestyle and budget accordingly, you can free yourself from the constraints of the modern world. You can say goodbye to financial problems and pervading feelings of denial. No longer will you be overwhelmed by desires that never seem to give you any satisfaction.

A minimalist budget is an approach to self-fulfillment and abundance that might seem counter-intuitive to most. This book will offer the bigger picture of what it means to budget. You will realize there is more to it than money management. You will also learn that when a life budget considers your behavioral, emotional, social and spiritual capital, you will make much better decisions.

We will talk about spending and shopping habits, identify problem areas, explore debt and how you can achieve your financial goals. You will look at ways you can put these principles into place and ensure that you stay motivated and focused. This book emphasizes the concept of minimalism instead of thriftiness. You aren't buying cheaply, you are minimizing the impulse to buy unnecessarily. That's right, even your cheap purchases need to go. They're doing more harm than you think!

If you can create a budget with a better understanding of your relationship with money and how it affects your lifestyle, the changes you apply will be long-lasting and truly authentic.

Minimalism isn't about surviving with less than you need. It's about identifying what you need and fulfilling the need completely without accumulating excess. Having exactly what you need is far from suffering. In fact, the excess in your life is responsible for more suffering than you even realize. Minimalist budgeting is about knowing what you need to have enough, and how best you can use your money to achieve that. When you approach your finances with this mindset, every penny is used efficiently and nothing is wasted.

We live a short life, and material goods and money can provide us with new ways to enjoy our life. They can assist us in moving closer to what we find worthwhile and meaningful. But that doesn't mean that they are worthwhile and meaningful in themselves. How we spend our money is an expression of what we think is crucial and our values, but in no way does it dictate the value or quality of our life. It gives us the illusion of determining our quality of life, and that's the problem. We are measuring happiness and satisfaction by the wrong standards – that's why we never feel we score very high.

How much would you be willing to pay for the calm and peace of mind achieved through living well? How much of your life do you lose when working? When it comes to expenses, do you remember to consider the time you wasted stressing about money? These questions might seem overly philosophical and vague, but they help us get to the root of how we make money, spend it and form a mentality around it. Once we've understood these roots, our efforts to save money will become much easier. We'll develop a more meaningful relationship with money, and this can mean the difference between scraping by and big savings that shape your future.

What will you learn after reading this book? You'll gain a deeper understanding of what makes a long-lasting budget. You will identify crucial and practical saving tips regarding matters of debt, children, cleaning, home, health, clothes, and food. You will also learn how to set realistic goals that match your personal budget. You will learn how to put everything you have learned into practice, come up with your own personal budget and much more.

The longer you cling to your current bad habits, the more difficult it becomes to shift your behavior and thinking. These money-wasting habits take root inside your subconscious and before you know it, it is second nature. To increase the likelihood of succeeding at minimalism and finally make big savings the new norm, it is vital that you start now. Stop wasting time. Stop making excuses. The longer you wait, the longer it is before you finally achieve your goals.

If you want to free yourself from your current financial constraints, then turn the page and read on. The techniques you'll unlock will make lasting, positive changes to your financial standing.

Chapter 1 – The Minimalist Budget Mindset

In recent years, the minimalism trend has become increasingly popular across the United States, particularly among the millennial generation. It has inspired a lot of people to downsize their possessions and live only with what they need. Aside from helping you declutter and destress, adopting a minimalist view of budgeting may also help you achieve financial freedom, releasing you from the shackles of a life lived paycheck to paycheck.

For one to have a minimalist budget, it's crucial to get into a minimalist mindset. It is the mindset of someone who chooses to live a minimalist life and ensure that this mindset becomes the root of all their behavior.

Most people who choose to simplify their life, do so because they begin thinking differently about how they can live a better life. Or perhaps they start to notice the destructive nature of their thoughtless consumerism, leading to a decided effort to make a change.

You need to cultivate the right mindset to ensure that your hard-earned money is spent well. Without the right mindset, the transition into minimalism is a much more difficult endeavor. You will try to resist temptations. You will try to reduce the amount of physical and mental clutter in your life. You will try to look for solutions. But as you try, the inner urges will continue to grow. Without the right mindset, you will find yourself relapsing. Any attempt at minimalism will only have you running back to satisfy your usual desires. This is why mental and emotional preparations are vital.

You may be wary of the idea of unfulfilled desires. This doesn't mean that you should give up on minimalism. In fact, the minimalist budget mindset is not about fighting your desires at all, it's about learning to stop desiring.

When you have cultivated the right mindset, you will realize that it is easy to live a simple life. Your motives will drive you and your actions will fall into place.

The budget mindset is best seen as a reduction of clutter based on your priorities. This doesn't mean you must get rid of or stop buying things that make you happy immediately. Minimization must be done at a reasonable pace. With time, you will begin to only seek out those things that are crucial.

Most people look to cut back on material possessions and objects, but when the minimalist mindset is involved, it applies to relationships and activities as well. After all, many areas of our life can be filled with excess.

Most people don't understand why someone would want to live a life within a minimalist budget. They don't understand how anyone could want to avoid luxuries.

They believe they should live however they want, and that is true. What these people don't understand is that living a minimalist life on a minimalist budget still allows you to do what you want. The things that you want are simply different. Living on a minimalist budget brings many benefits. It's just that most people are not aware of them.

The money mindset encompasses the thoughts and feelings you subconsciously develop toward money from life experiences. Since our thoughts control our actions, developing a negative mindset when it comes to money can create a huge barrier between you and financial health. It can result in stress and anxiety, and it will hinder you from reaching your financial goals.

But developing a negative money mindset doesn't mean you will always feel that way. Read on to learn how you can develop the right mindset to help you achieve your financial goals.

How to dramatically shift your thinking from a negative to positive mindset when it comes to money

Most people know what they're supposed to do when money management is involved – save funds for an emergency, spend less than the money they earn and invest for retirement. But developing other good habits is crucial. Managing money requires discipline and discipline doesn't come automatically; you must learn and teach yourself to abide by your own goals.

Your success in managing money depends on how you think about money. If you want to eliminate financial stress from your life or get better at money management, it's vital that you change how you think about money and develop a positive money mindset. It applies to every aspect of life. You need to make a positive change in everything you do to be successful. This will help you change what and how you talk.

Speaking and thinking more positively will make a huge difference, but it also requires action. It is essential that you change how you've been doing things, and take steps in a new direction for real and lasting change.

During times of hardship, such as after the death or loss of a partner, it can seem challenging to develop a positive mindset about anything. And not just about money. You might experience even more financial difficulties after this loss. Or perhaps you aren't short of money, but you have no knowledge about how to handle your finances, and this makes you nervous about the future.

Stress due to finances can come from anywhere, and it might become worse when grief or trauma are involved.

Fortunately, there are many steps you can take to dramatically shift your mindset from negative to positive, and develop great habits. Here are the steps you can take:

1. Forgive yourself for financial mistakes you've made

You won't find anyone who has never missed a bill or credit card payment. Everyone has spent some of their savings in the spur of the moment. Virtually all adults have made these same mistakes, and that's why you should forgive yourself.

When you forgive yourself for past mistakes, it will set you free. You will make room for a healthy attitude and better practices for saving money. Stop focusing on guilt and start focusing on progress.

2. Know your money mindset

You may think you understand your attitude towards money, but chances are you're not fully aware of how your mindset affects your decision-making. It's recommended that you track the thoughts that cross your mind every time you make a decision concerning money. What type of items do you find yourself reaching for? What problems do you imagine they will solve? What events in your life trigger these desires?

Since we make a lot of these decisions in our lives, you should do this for at least one whole day and examine the results. Look for patterns that give you a clue about your attitude.

Once you come to a better understanding about your mindset, it will be easy to identify habits and beliefs that prevent you from abiding by plans and goals.

3. Don't compare yourself to others

In the age of reality TV, celebrity magazines and social media, it's easy to make comparisons. We compare ourselves to celebrities, friends, family members and even fictional characters on television. You need to quit this bad habit for a few reasons:

• You're comparing what you know about yourself to only what you see of somebody else. What you're comparing yourself to is the best side of someone's life. What you see in the media is carefully curated for the public and in no way reflective of reality.

• You don't know the details of the other people's finances. Some might live a luxurious life, but it's likely many of these people are also paying off credit card debt.

• After comparing yourself to others, you'll be filled with feelings of inadequacy. This will divert attention from your aspirations and finances, slowing further progress.

Therefore, you should create achievable goals, and measure your success this way. Celebrate the wins and keep your goals updated when you achieve them.

4. Create good habits and maintain them

Once you've established realistic goals, it's good to develop the habits that will help you achieve them. If you've never looked at your expenses in detail or created a budget, then perhaps it's time to do so. When you understand how you're spending money, it can be easy to figure out where you can save.

It'll help you create attainable goals which, step by step, will lead you towards success. One effective habit is following a set time to review your finances and check on progress. If you are in a relationship, choose a time that works for both of you and make sure you're both present.

Even if one partner is appointed to be the money manager, ensure that both parties are on the same page and agree to arranged goals to avoid miscommunication. When you have a clear picture of your financial situation, you can discuss how to delegate money.

5. Become a money mindset sponge

One of the easiest ways to build a good money mindset is to surround yourself with people who live by the values you most admire. When you spend time with people that have a good mindset around money, you will actively learn from them, and you will naturally adapt to their qualities over time.

You can also look for free content online as there are a lot of experts that speak on these topics through live streams, podcasts, and YouTube videos. Consider digesting an hour's worth of money mindset content every day.

Taking this simple step will drastically change your perspective and begin eliminating those limiting beliefs that hold you back from achieving your goals. Changing the people that surround you will change your life.

6. Identify your go-to affirmations for daily empowerment

Find five one-liners that you can repeat daily to center yourself, keep you aligned with your financial goals, and inspire you to make leaps towards success.

For instance, if you struggle with the idea that people with money are greedy, then you're likely engaging in subconscious self-sabotage by keeping a low-paying job. The ideal affirmation for you should be a reminder that having money and being a good person are two different things. Keep telling yourself that you'll give back more to the world when you have more money.

If you grew up feeling that money is scarce and that only some people are entitled to it, then you need to remind yourself there's unlimited money and it's coming your way because you deserve it.

Write down powerful affirmations and keep them in places such as your car dashboard, your wallet, on your bathroom mirror or your smartphone lock screen. Keep reading them out loud. It might seem ridiculous at first, but after some time, you'll start to believe them. Repetition will lead to results, and everything you concentrate on will start to manifest into reality.

7. Ditch negative language

Perhaps you've noticed that most people spend a lot of their time complaining. Sometimes it can be the easiest way to bond with someone, break an awkward silence, or get some cheap gratification.

Most negative conversations revolve around four topics: a bad relationship, work complaints, a bad financial situation, or bad health.

If you engage in these conversations often, you need to stop and concentrate on your dreams. You can't have both excuses and the results at the same time. When you allow unrestricted negative ideas to flow out of your mouth, you can fall into a sense of self-pity and self-victimization. These feelings will prevent you from taking powerful action, and hold you back from your goals.

Eliminate negative language from your self-talk and see everything as an opportunity for growth. Positive language might seem cheesy at first, but it leads to positive beliefs that will attract positive outcomes.

8. Get the right mentors

Think about who you take advice from. Is it your partner? Your parents? Your co-workers? While they may have some interesting insights, they're not always the most helpful mentors.

Challenge yourself to seek advice from those who have already achieved the goals you are trying to achieve. This means you need to get clear about what you want. Do you want your business to make more money? Do you want a new job? Do you want to completely pay off your debt? Don't just seek out those who are close to you; seek out those you are most interested in emulating.

Reflect on what you want, seek out those mentors, and prepare to spend a lot of time learning from them.

9. Practice gratitude

Daily gratitude has proven powerful. You can start by writing down three things you are grateful for each day. Check your gratitude journal every time you are overwhelmed or feeling negative about your finances. This will give you a positive boost. Studies have shown that gratitude practices can actually rewire the brain to feel happiness more often. The more happy you are, the less likely you are to give into your bad spending habits.

10. Learn and implement new knowledge

Being educated on financial matters will help you feel confident and in control of the future. Consider finding the right education for yourself. Different approaches work best for different people. Explore and discover the financial education that suits you best.

You will find books, experts, and educational platforms that offer a range of different approaches. Education is crucial to maintaining a positive money mindset.

Free yourself from a Consumerist Mindset

Most of the world's population has a consumerist mindset. It doesn't just refer to the omnipresence of advertising, but everything related to the idea that we must own more stuff to be better, more successful, or happier people. This mindset is pervasive in today's culture.

We must emphasize that this consumerist belief is not based in any truth. Owning less brings more benefits than owning more. Freedom from a consumerist mindset brings:

- **More freedom from comparison** – You'll be liberated

from constant comparisons to other people's lives. No longer will your mind be fraught with envy, looking at what other people have versus what you don't. Constant comparisons can make us depressed and unable to enjoy what we have. Without this in our lives, you'll feel far more secure than you ever have before.

• **More time and opportunities to pursue other things** – Most material things fade, spoil, and perish. But joy, love, purpose, and compassion stand eternal. Our lives are better lived pursuing them. Being less preoccupied with possessions offers this opportunity. Once you clear your life of meaningless objects and expenses, you will have a lot more money and energy to focus on what truly makes you happy.

• **Less debt** – Money that would have gone towards buying pointless new things can now be invested in more important areas of your life. Owning less allows you to finally start saving money and pay off debt.

• **Less stress** – Many people don't realize this, but it can be stressful to own things you no longer use or care about. This can be guilt-induced stress or stress from maintaining the object. Sometimes these useless possessions can even get in the way. The more objects we own, the more stuff we have to break, and the more money we have to spend to maintain or repair the object. Less possessions means less stuff to worry about.

• **Reduced symptoms of depression** – There is evidence to show that consumerism can increase the likelihood of depression and make symptoms worse. This is because consumerism convinces us there's a lack or void that needs to be filled with material goods. This can create feelings of depression, especially since this void does not exist, so nothing we do can change the way we feel. By defending ourselves against the forces that try to create this dissatisfaction, we will feel much more fulfilled in our daily lives. This is who we really are without consumerism in our lives.

•   **Gratitude and contentment**– The easiest way to feel satisfied is to appreciate what you have. It's only natural that when you have less, you appreciate what you have even more. You are more likely to care for and maintain belongings when you don't have as much to worry about.

Breaking from compulsive consumerism is an important step towards a simplified life. How, then, do we achieve this freedom? What are the required steps to break free? Here is a helpful guide for achieving freedom from a consumerist mindset.

1.   Admit it's possible

It's important to break out of the mindset that the way you live now is the only way you can live. Recognize the lifestyle you're used to is only that – the lifestyle you're used to. It is not the lifestyle you need to be happy. A lot of people throughout history adopted a minimalist lifestyle that rejected and overcame consumerism. Find motivation in how these impressive figures did it. This will help you realize that you, too, can find the same success. The journey to victory starts when you admit it's possible.

2.   Adopt a traveler's mentality

When traveling, people only take what they need for that journey. This ensures that we feel freer, lighter and more flexible. We pack the essentials we can't live without and we realize that all excess creates more stress down the road.

The adoption of a traveler's mindset has the same benefits for life as it does for travel. You'll feel less weighed down, and yet you'll still have everything you need. A traveler's mindset will also prevent you from spending money on items that are unnecessary.

3. Embrace the benefits of owning less

People don't usually think of the benefits of owning less, but there are many. When these practical benefits are articulated, it becomes easy to understand, recognize and desire. As soon the lifestyle change is made, you can expect to feel inundated with minimalism's benefits, including a stronger sense of lightness and freedom. Instead of focusing on the things you're giving up, start thinking about all the new benefits that will enter your life.

4. Be aware of consumerist tactics

The world will make you believe that the best way to contribute to society is by spending your money. We are swarmed by advertisements every day trying to convince us to buy more and more. Recognizing the consumerist tactics in our world will not make them go away, but they can help you understand when a desire has simply been manufactured by a well-designed advertisement. Many products that are on the market today don't really solve any problem for us. We are convinced we want it because we have been bombarded by images and videos telling us we want it. But think about it this way: if you had never seen the advertisement, would you have really sat at home wishing that the product existed? Probably not. This is a clear sign of a manufactured desire.

5.   Compare down instead of up

When we start comparing our lives to people around us, we lose contentment, joy, and happiness. We begin focusing all our attention on eliminating this difference. That's because we tend to compare upward, only looking at people who have more than us. We must break the consumerism trap by taking notice of those who have less than us. This will help us remain joyful and grateful for what we currently have.

6.   Consider the full cost of what you buy

When we purchase items, we tend to only look at the sticker price. But the number on the tag is not the full cost. What we buy always costs us extra energy, time, and focus. This also includes fixing, maintaining, organizing, cleaning, removing and replacing. Make a habit of considering these expenses before making a purchase. You'll find yourself making wiser and more confident decisions when it comes to money.

7.   Turn off the TV

Corporations spend a huge amount of money on advertising because they know they can make consumers buy their products or services this way. Television is an industry built on the assumption that you can be persuaded to spend money on nearly anything. No one is immune and even if you don't realize it, TV has likely convinced you to buy something you normally wouldn't have. When you reduce the amount of time you spend watching TV, you are less likely to be persuaded to buy items you don't need.

8.   Make gratitude a part of your life

Gratitude helps us to respond positively to our life circumstances and change our attitude during times of stress.

Make it part of your life during the hardships, as well as periods of abundance. Start focusing on the blessings and not just your troubles. Studies have shown that gratitude practices increase our sense of happiness.

9.   Practice generosity

Giving helps us to recognize how much we are blessed with and what else we have to offer. It allows us to find fulfillment and purpose in assisting others. When we act generously, we take on a mindset of abundance, and this can assist us in embracing minimalism. When we give to others, we begin to believe subconsciously that we have a lot more to spare.

It's worth noting that generosity leads us to contentment, and not the other way around. We should not wait to be content before acting generously.

10.   Renew your commitment daily

Everywhere we go, we are flooded with advertisements. At times, it can almost feel overwhelming. We must continue to reject these consumerist ideologies and remain strong in the face of destructive excess. For total freedom, we must cultivate self-awareness and recommit ourselves to our goals every day. The best part is, the more we continue to commit ourselves, the easier it becomes. Soon this commitment to a better life becomes your new norm.

Quick Start Action Steps to free yourself from Compulsive Spending once and for all

At some point or another, we've all been caught up in excessive spending and its destructive cycle. Despite our best intentions, sometimes it can be hard to stop impulse purchases. And as soon as we start spending impulsively, it can be challenging to keep our finances on track. Every purchase is on the spur of the moment, and our actions are no longer conscious.

Although not formally recognized by medical research, compulsive spending is a serious issue, and it has been on the rise for the past few years. Your spending becomes compulsive when it's out of control, excessive and results in legal, social, or financial problems. But even if your consequences aren't as extreme, compulsive spending could still be a major issue you need to quit. Do you frequently make purchases that you can't really afford, yet you make them anyway? That is a problem, my friend.

Some people view spending as a confidence booster, as they think that buying new things makes them seem more glamorous and prosperous than they are. And of course, the public is inundated by billboards, print ads, commercials, and other advertisements to entice anyone with a compulsive spending habit. You think this way because big corporations want you to think this way.

To prevent needless purchases, you should know what you are shopping for and stay focused on exactly what it is you've set out to do. This is a sure way to safeguard against overspending.

If your finances are getting out of hand, you can regain some control with this step-by-step plan. Remember, money doesn't have to slip through your fingers!

1. Get to the root of the problem

Compulsive spenders accumulate a lot of stuff, but that's not the root of the problem. You must consider what you are really buying. Above all, compulsive spending is a response to an emotional problem. We feel some level of unrest or emptiness, and somehow, we have become convinced that a new purchase is the solution.

A person might be dealing with anxiety, depression, anger, or grief. These emotions can trigger spending, which may result in shame, fear, guilt, feelings of inadequacy, doubt, and many others.

You should identify your triggers and attempt to get them under control. It is recommended to seek professional therapy or support groups to help you manage your spending problem.

You should also consider talking to a friend, and sometimes they can be great therapists.

2.   Pay in cash

People tend to spend more when they are paying with debit cards and credit cards. It's no wonder why. Charging bills to a piece of plastic can make you feel disconnected from money. It's easier to ignore what the cost means for your financial situation, and this can easily result in overspending.

Spending feels real when you take dollars out from your wallet. Start setting aside a portion of your income expressly for bills and withdrawing the rest in cash.

Chances are that you will not go on a compulsive spending binge since you can understand more acutely that you have a limited amount of money.

3.   Give your purchases a score

Give every item you purchase a score based on how necessary it is to you. The more necessary it is, the higher the score. When you look back at your purchases, you'll see how much you can save by removing the unnecessary purchases. By eliminating low-scoring items, you'll be surprised by how much you can save.

Without scoring the items you buy, it can be difficult to know which purchases matter to you the most. Sooner or later you'll run low on money, with an excess of low-scoring items and possibly a lack of the high-scoring things you truly need.

When it comes to scoring items, you must be honest with yourself. Don't give something a higher score just because you really want it. Really consider how necessary it is. Can something else you own perform the same function? Will the quality of your life really suffer without it?

4. Wait at least 20 minutes before buying anything

When you spot an object you want to buy, your body takes over your mind and it can be difficult to think rationally. To avoid the urge to spend, try waiting for at least 20 minutes before making a purchase. Tell yourself that you can only make the purchase the item if you still feel it's necessary once you've walked away from it. After that time, you may realize you don't really want the item and resist the spending urge. When we are no longer faced with the item in question, it's easier for us to say no.

5. Find social connections

Compulsive spenders waste their money on material goods because they are trying to fill the need for human connection with shopping. The truth is, you can never have enough of the things you don't need. That's why you should learn to fill your life with activities and social connections instead. These activities can involve clubs, learning a new skill, charity groups, or sports.

Many people see shopping as the center of their social life, but it does not have to be this way. When you fill your life with new, meaningful experiences, there will be changes in how you spend and improved satisfaction overall.

6. Pay attention to your spending patterns

You need to know where your money is going. Track how you spend for a month and look for a trend. You might be surprised by the amount of money you lose on insignificant activities like lunch out or frequent coffees.

Take note of your necessary expenses and list them as your priorities. These include:

- Shelter and utilities

- Food

- Transportation

- Basic clothing

All this said, your necessities are no reason to splurge. You don't have to buy new clothes every week or go out to dinner every night. Check your monthly expenses so that you can find ways to trim the spending. Do you need that fancy satellite dish when you can stream your favorite shows on the internet? What about the $40 gym membership you haven't used in five months? Questions like this will help you stay on the path to healthy spending.

7. Spend money with a purpose

After putting together a monthly budget, create a spending plan to go along with it.

If you need concert tickets or new clothes, ensure that you add them to their budget categories after prioritizing your necessities.

You only need to withdraw the cash you need and sort it into labeled envelopes. For instance, if you choose to allocate $200 every month for groceries, set aside $100 after you receive the first paycheck and have it in a groceries envelope. Add the remaining amount when you get the second paycheck.

If your line of work has an unpredictable cash flow, consider creating a budget for irregular income.

You can use a free budgeting app to create your budget in no time. It will help you plan, monitor your debt, track your spending and monitor your saving process.

8. Shop with a goal

We've all bought things that we didn't plan. You go to the supermarket and all you need is toothpaste and shampoo, but as soon as you walk through the door, you end up filling your basket with stuff you'll probably only use once. A short trip to the store can become expensive when you're a compulsive spender.

No one plans to get sidetracked when they're shopping, but if you often find yourself spending needless amounts of money, consider planning your trip beforehand. As long as you stick to your plan, you won't have to worry about overspending.

9. Don't spend money on eating out

Changing your spending habits on food is an efficient way to cut down expenses. Many don't realize it, but dining out can get expensive very fast. If you spend $20 on lunch four times a week, it will cost you $80 per week and $320 per month.

Instead of eating out every day, make a meal plan for one week and buy the required groceries at the store. Make sure to bring a list so you only purchase what you intend to use for your home-cooked meals.

Lunchtime offers a perfect opportunity to cut back. Consider bringing lunch to work every day. Make it simple. Prepare meals on Sundays or take about twenty minutes every night to prepare a sandwich.

This doesn't mean you shouldn't treat yourself, it just means you need to stick to your budget. After all, you can still make delicious and cost-effective homemade meals.

10. Resist sales

We all love a good deal. Retailers understand this well and they know how flashy sales are irresistible to their customers. Sometimes a big sale can even get people to purchase items they don't really want; they just can't resist the deal, no matter how useless what they're buying is.

If you've ever bought something you didn't mean to buy just because it's 30% off, it means you paid 70% more than you intended. That's not saving money at all; you're still spending. It is essential that you start to practice self-discipline when you see a sale at the store. Remind yourself that keeping all your money is far better than saving 30%.

11. Challenge yourself to achieve new goals

Strengthen your willpower by giving yourself new challenges. For example, try only to purchase your necessities for a month. You'll be surprised by how little you need.

This will also give you a chance to identify what you don't really need. Do you like paying for your monthly gym membership because it helps you stay active? Then keep it. Do you like going to a chiropractor because it keeps your back in good shape? Keep going. If it fits into the budget and is good for you, then keep enjoying it.

Chapter 2 - Start Saving Money

Do you ever wonder where that money goes? Do you earn a lot of money but still live paycheck to paycheck? Do you sometimes look at your savings and feel like you could do better?

If the answer to any of these questions is 'yes,' then you are not alone. You'd be surprised by the number high-income individuals who can't seem to save a penny. They spend with the mindset that there's lots of money to spare. Funnily enough, they end up having none of it to spare. It doesn't matter how much money you have; if you never spend responsibly, your bank balances will be much lower than they should be.

Most people who live paycheck to paycheck blame their finance issues on lifestyle purchases such as entertainment and dining. Most claim their lack of discipline continues to prevent them from achieving their goals. Their money is lost on things that could be avoided with a little extra effort and creativity.

If you want to achieve your financial goals, you must learn more about your spending habits, create foolproof plans to save money, and cultivate self-discipline in the face of temptation. How do you achieve all this? Let's discuss them individually.

Figure out where the heck all your money goes every month

It's good to have a budget, but if you aren't tracking your expenses, you'll lose track of this budget easily, defeating its entire purpose. You'll run the risk of setting unrealistic goals that you never meet. It is only when you discover where your money is going that you have a good idea of what to cut down. Many people are surprised at what they spend the most money on. You may think it's too many subscription services, but what if it's actually the $5 latte you have five days of the week?

This is the cycle that most people fall into. If you want to make a change, tracking your spending is a must. Here is how it works:

Steps to track your expenses

1. Create a budget

You need a budget to track your expenses. Without one, it would be a difficult challenge to work out what the biggest drain on your money is. A budget shows your expected income and all expenses by category.

A budget doesn't control you; you adjust it as you please. It serves as a guide to ensure your money does what you tell it to do.

There are three steps to creating a budget:

• Write down your monthly income.

• Write down your monthly expenses.

a) Start with shelter, food, transportation, and clothing.

b) When the necessities are covered, list other expenses like eating out, TV streaming services, savings, gym memberships, etc.

• Ensure that your income minus expenses comes to zero.

31

2. Record your expenses

Keep a record of your expenses every day. In a small notepad or your phone's Notes app, jot down everything you spend money on, from your morning cup of coffee to that new pair of shoes. If you fail to keep up with what you spend, you'll feel like you're in a fantasy land where money never runs out. This would be great – except it isn't the real world. Money does run out, and when it does, those consequences can hit you hard.

3. Watch those numbers

Make sure that when you note down your expenses, you track how much is left in the category. This way you'll have a better idea of when the cost of something is too high.

If you are married, talk with your partner and ensure you both record all spending that takes place. Make sure to check in with each other before spending. This practice is excellent for igniting great communication and accountability.

Budgets are blown when you fail to track and watch how you spend.

4 Ways to track your expenses

As we've demonstrated, tracking your expenses is a very important practice. There are also many ways that you can do it. Each method comes with its own advantages and disadvantages. Finding which one suits you best can shape your entire experience of budgeting, determining whether this habit becomes a permanent part of your lifestyle or not. Feel free to try each one out to see for yourself.

1. Paper and pencil

Old-school methods are still extremely helpful. Many people prefer to keep track of their budget on paper. The benefit of physical writing is that it requires an active brain. An active brain will remember more clearly what was written down, so all numbers in the budget are always carefully considered. Using ink and paper also means you can use gel pens and other coloring tools that can make your expense-tracking more fun. The bright colors might even make your task feel less daunting.

The downside to this method is that most of us don't keep paper copies anymore. When you receive a receipt, you must hold onto it until the budget is updated. It's also more difficult to make amendments if you discover you recorded something inaccurately.

You'll likely find yourself misplacing receipts. Sometimes you simply forget to ask for one. Sometimes certain purchases don't get written down. Any of these issues can lead to problematic tracking. And if you lose your expense-tracking sheet, it'll be a big drag to start all over.

2. The envelope system

This method involves paying cash in person. You can create special allocations for utilities, mortgage, and retirement. You can make a debit card payment online or send checks for other utilities. But the expenses you pay in person should only be in cash.

At the beginning of the month, place cash in envelopes labeled with the budget lines. Eating out, entertainment and groceries are the three perfect examples. Remember to carry the groceries envelope with you whenever you go to a grocery store. When the envelope is empty, that's when you stop spending. Using this method, your money will essentially be tracking itself.

Well, the truth is, paying in cash can sometimes be inconvenient. Who likes keeping up with coins or counting out bills? Who wants to go inside a gas station to prepay at the register? Plus, with the recent increase in e-commerce, cash payment options aren't always available. However, this is a great way to track your expenses. That's because watching the envelope become empty will inspire a new level of responsibility.

3. Computer spreadsheets

Many people have gone digital and most of them are spreadsheet fanatics. They love discussing spreadsheet perks, and if you don't know what they're talking about, you probably couldn't care less. The reality is, however, that spreadsheets offer plenty of benefits. This includes the ability to customize your budget, use a plethora of templates, and last but not least, all the math is done for you.

Unfortunately, spreadsheet enthusiasts don't always find a fellow spreadsheet enthusiast. It's likely that only one partner will want to use it. Couples should communicate openly about their preferences. You shouldn't let spreadsheets come between a happy marriage.

Another problem with spreadsheets is getting your computer to keep up with the spending. If you fail to log these expenses daily, your budget won't be a budget at all, just a spreadsheet with good but empty intentions. We all have good intentions in the beginning, but they don't accomplish financial goals on their own.

It's probable that you spend a decent amount of time on the computer, so perhaps spreadsheets will work for you. But do you know what else will always be at your side? Your phone. That brings us to the next and best option for tracking expenses.

4. Budgeting apps

There are a lot of free budgeting apps that will create a budget in just a few minutes. You can easily log in to your phone and enter your expenses the moment they occur. You won't have to go about your day, risking forgetfulness about your budget updates.

That's how convenient a budgeting app is. Some of these apps let you customize your templates to meet your saving and spending goals. The best part is you can sync your budget with your partner's devices and be in constant commerce communication.

No matter the method you choose, make tracking your expenses a habit if you want to achieve your financial goals. If you fail to track your money, you will always be wondering where your money went. But with the right tools and self-discipline, you can achieve financial victories.

11 simple ways to instantly start saving money

You work hard to earn your money, so it should also work hard for you. Intentionality is the key to making your money go the extra mile. Being intentional is how you'll start saving more and spending less each month. When we are intentional with our money, we know where each penny is going. Every time we swipe our credit card or pull a bill out of our wallet, we are aware of why we are doing it and it is not done out of impulse.

This, in turn, keeps more of our money in our account.

There are a lot of ways to save money. Where do you start? Start easy. Start quick. Start here. These are 8 simple tips to help you save money every day, week, month, or year. Here they are:

1. Get cheaper alternatives

If you want to save money, reduce what you spend. There are ways to do this so you still get what you need, but at a much smaller cost. For instance, if you love shopping, consider taking advantage of coupons. You can save money by using cash back or coupons from money-saving apps. Many will let you know about the best prices available on certain items. You can download these apps from your favorite stores and there are a lot of ways you can save money by using them. You can check out sales, nab coupons and join reward programs. Just make sure to resist the temptation to shop online.

You can also look for other alternatives by getting used items. Instead of getting a new item, you can get something used but still in good condition at a lower price. When it comes to buying used items, your discretion is required. Some things cannot be bought used like tires and a toothbrush. But if you're looking for a car, books, video games, tools, or pets, then you can save a lot of money by buying gently used items.

If you love exercising and currently pay for a gym membership, consider other means like finding workout videos online. Some people need the human interaction we get at the gym, while others prefer to lose weight without a membership, special class fees, and a personal trainer. If you want to burn calories without incurring huge monthly expenses, consider exercise-streaming services and YouTube videos. Many fitness gurus have realized that we need non-DVD options we can use at home, and they are creating high-quality content that we can enjoy anytime from the comfort of our home.

Aside from these options, you can also consider brewing your own coffee instead of buying it, and you can cook at home instead of paying for meals at a restaurant. If you spend about $5 per day on your favorite barista blend, it would cost you $35 per week and about $150 per month. Instead of this, you can spend just $20 a month brewing your own and you'll save $130. You can put these savings towards greater things like your dream vacation, retirement, a sinking fund, or whatever your goals are financially.

Instead of paying for an expensive form of entertainment, consider free options. How about e-books, audiobooks, physical books, movies, performances or presentations? Where do you get all of this? At a local library, of course. Get a library card now!

Save money and still have fun.

2. Eliminate the things you don't need

You can save a significant amount of money by eliminating goods, subscriptions, and other services that you don't really need. Do you really need different music and TV streaming services? How many subscription magazines or boxes show up in your mail each month? I am not saying you should avoid these services, but if you haven't thought about them in a while, chances are that you're subscribed to services you don't use, read or watch any more. If you want to save some money, cut out any monthly subscriptions that you no longer have use for.

You can also make further eliminations by evaluating your TV choices. If you pay high cable package prices and only end up watching a few channels, then you are not alone. A lot of people are realizing they can save a large amount of money and still watch the shows they want by choosing other options.

Consider Vimeo, YouTube, Amazon Prime Video, Netflix, or Hulu. Consider watching recently aired episodes online. Or try using that library card.

You don't have to return to medieval times where the only entertainment was watching a joust. You just have to trade that cable bill for a cheaper but equally awesome option.

3. Eliminate expense-increasing practices

Don't wait for expenses to accumulate before making a change. For starters, consider making more energy-efficient life choices. Some of these might require big initial investments, but they pay off in the end. To save on home expenses, turn off the lights when you leave home, buy energy-saving light bulbs, take quick showers and purchase a programmable thermostat.

To save on transportation costs, use public transportation, carpool, or consider biking. These green options will do wonders for your savings as well as the planet.

If you're considering buying a video game console, think twice. Having a console only means you'll want to spend more money on games. This is an expensive purchase that will only lead to even more expensive purchases.

You should also avoid credit cards so you don't find yourself getting into debt. A great first step to getting ahead is to stop getting behind. That sounds logical, doesn't it? Credit cards are easy ways to fall behind. After all, this is how you accumulate debt in the first place. Debt gives us the illusion of ownership.

It keeps out the sunshine of true ownership, however, as it's like a grey, hovering cloud of obligation.

Stop using credit cards, and you will start owning for real. Instead of making debt payments, how about make savings? Not only is this an empowering life change, but you'll thank yourself for it later.

Once you've gotten rid of credit cards, consider removing your debit card information from online shops. The quickest way to spend money these days is through the "one-click" feature. This is when websites store your payment information and make purchases far too easy with a single click of a button. When buying is so easy, overspending is extremely likely. Take your time to retrieve your wallet, pull out your debit card, and do the tedious job of entering all the numbers. As you are going about this arduous process, consider whether this purchase is worth it. Imagine yourself making that transaction and how it will affect your budget. If you still think it's a good idea after thinking it through, then go ahead as you intended.

You can also reduce your future expenses by performing a maintenance check on household objects, such as appliances and cars. Most of these things can be very expensive when replacing or repairing, and a monthly routine check can save you from future financial headaches. Have your car cleaned, checked, and fill the air in the tires when needed. Clean out home vents and remember to check any wear and tear on appliances.

Sometimes a simple bolt, washer, screw replacement, or cleaning can keep it running efficiently.

Before you shop, you should always give it some thought. You don't want to incur huge expenses for something you won't use.

Always sleep on a huge decision before taking the plunge. Perhaps even, take a few days. Take the time to check on prices, compare their advantages and disadvantages, and perform desire measuring.

What is desire measuring, you ask? You think you want that trendy, weather-proof laptop case the moment you see it. But does the desire reduce with time? Impulse buying can be expensive. Practice patience to avoid running your wallet dry.

4. Spend creatively

If you want to save money and still get what you want, consider creative ways to find a balance. For instance, a date doesn't have to be expensive to be exciting. There's this pervasive myth that spending a lot of money on a date will guarantee you the love of your life. The truth is, money has nothing to do with it. You can fall in love and have fun while still adhering to minimalist practices.

Consider filling a picnic basket with apples, popcorn, chocolate, and an assortment of cheeses. You can also bring home Chinese takeout and eat while you watch your favorite show. Or how about hanging out at the park? There are many ways to enjoy a date without making your bank account suffer. And if your date can't enjoy the simple things in life, is this really someone you want to see permanently? You might find that minimalism opens your eyes to all the shallow and superficial people in your life. Good riddance!

Consider engaging in more outdoor activities for fun. These activities can offer great entertainment and most don't require a lot of money. There are plenty of things about nature to find fascinating. Consider biking, hiking, spiking, backpacking, kayaking, stargazing, corn-mazing, or curtain-raising. Get out, have fun and save up.

5. Sell what you don't need

Clutter can give us the illusion of completion, but it is the furthest thing from it. Clutter is made up of stuff that nobody really needs. It can be a drain on your energy, overwhelming corners, closets, and drawers all over your house. Having clutter in your vicinity can cloud your sense of clarity. Catching sight of overflowing cupboards may make you feel like your mind, too, is overflowing.

You can cash in by selling the items that you don't need. Post about them online, take them to a consignment shop, or have an old-fashioned garage sale. There are also numerous apps that provide an inviting and fun platform for others to purchase second-hand items. For clothes, try using Vinted, and for all used books, why not hop on Amazon?

Reduce the number of possessions you don't need, create a calmer home environment, and make cash while you do it.

6. Get excited about borrowing instead of buying

Chances are, if there's something you really need temporarily, someone you know already owns it. Perhaps you're going to a black-tie event and you don't own the right kind of blazer. Perhaps you're looking for a new book to read. Before heading to the store and pulling out your wallet, why not ask your friends if they have something you can borrow? There's a high likelihood they have something you can use. This means you have exactly what you need, and you get to save yourself some money and some extra clutter. Borrowing can be exciting! You can make anyone's stuff your stuff temporarily, and you don't need to pay for it. Just make sure to give it back in good condition as soon as you no longer need it.

7. Take advantage of offers and promos

Businesses provide all kinds of offers to their customers. Try to take advantage of these offers and save money this way. For example, when you're at a restaurant, take advantage of the happy hour specials. These days it extends to meals and not just drinks.

You should also consider eating apps. Subscribe for newsletters from your favorite restaurants, and they'll send you promos and coupons. By eating at a lower cost, you'll save money. And consider unsubscribing from stores or restaurants that tend to make you overspend. This requires some awareness of your spending patterns.

Check the bottom of your receipts as certain restaurants may offer discounts if you take a survey. You can make big savings in exchange for some of your time.

You can also hit up weekly ads and BOGOs. Stores with BOGO offers are practically begging you to save some money. Follow this money-saving move: create a meal plan based on your store's sales. Consider stocking up the freezer and pantry for the future. Keep in mind what you bought when making meal plans, for the future.

8. Make a shopping list and stick to your budget

Begin by planning your meals – decide on what you will eat at dinner, lunch, and breakfast for a whole week. Then make a list of the individual groceries you'll need to make those meals happen, keeping in mind your budget. You may find that purchasing separate ingredients is more cost-effective than buying many premade meals. Regardless of your preference, always stick to the list you make. This will keep you from overspending and forgetting items in your grocery budget.

9. Always ask for fees to be waived

When signing up for something, there may be some fees that are involved, and we always end up paying it. You'd be surprised how accommodating certain companies can be when you ask for a fee waiver.

In a recent survey conducted, it was found that over half of responders were successful in getting a bank or other financial institution to waive a fee. The most common fees to get waived are overdraft fees, followed closely by late payment fees.

Doing that won't make you rich, but some extra cash from waived fees can still be helpful. Not all companies will agree to this, but it never hurts to ask. Just make sure to explain your situation honestly and you find yourself being met with a compassionate fee waiver.

10. Skip the cheap stuff for lasting purchases

Buying cheaper items may save you money in the short-term, but if you want long-term savings, avoid them. It's no secret that cheap stuff tends to be lower in quality. What does that mean? Fragile items that are a lot more breakable. Once it breaks, you'll have to replace it. And that means spending yet more money on a replacement. If you continue to buy something cheap, this cycle will only continue. Eventually, you'll find you've spent a large amount of money on a dozen low-quality things, when you could have spent less money on one high-quality thing. To improve your savings, only purchase items that you know will last.

11. Say a permanent 'no' to one-time-use items

If you're only going to use the item once, do not purchase it. This only applies to non-food items, of course. Were you invited to a 20's themed party but you don't have any 20's themed clothes? You're probably thinking you should head to the store right now to buy a whole new outfit, but this is the opposite of what you should do. This will result not only in clutter, but needless money-spending. Do not purchase items you don't see yourself using for the rest of your life. A better option? Borrow the clothes. They'll be free if you borrow them from someone you know, or at the very least, cheaper than something brand new if you find a store that loans what you need.

How to develop self-discipline to stop yourself from overspending

We start off every month with the intention to save money, by only buying the things we need, staying away from sales displays, and watching our spending closely. Despite our best efforts, we may still find ourselves spending more than we wanted. Sometimes it can even feel like money just slips through our fingers.

Don't beat yourself up, this happens to most of us. There are many reasons why we might overspend. Sometimes it's because we aren't aware of our spending habits. Or because we've estimated our income, debt payments, and expenses incorrectly. This leads to the numbers in our bank account dipping lower than they should. Whatever the reason, if you're ready to take control of your money, here are some useful tips you can apply to develop the personal discipline to stop overspending.

1. Know your spending triggers

To develop self-discipline around spending, you must identify the physical and emotional triggers that make you spend. Once you're aware of these triggers, you can begin to eliminate the opportunity and temptation to overspend. Keep in mind:

Time of the day – Do you have more energy during certain periods of the day? If that's the case, shop only when you have more energy. This way, you'll make wise spending choices. After all, we can think much clearly when we're less pressured and more relaxed.

Environment – Are there certain environments that make you feel like spending? Shopping malls, craft fairs, home shows, and holidays are some examples of occasions on which you're likely to spend impulsively.

You can fight the temptation by taking less money with you or avoiding such environments.

Additionally, if you have a favorite store and sometimes you find yourself wandering through the aisles looking for amazing deals, try to limit the number of times you go there. If you simply can't limit your visits, keep your credit card and money safe from yourself, or ask someone you trust to do it for you.

Mood – Different emotional states and moods can change our energetic resources, making us overspend. For instance, if we're anxious, stressed or upset, we may take retail therapy a little too far. Instead of going to the mall, try hitting up the park or the gym. Exercise and fresh air will do wonders for improving your mood.

It is important to identify the moods that result in your bad shopping habits. Once these moods strike, go somewhere your wallet doesn't need to be involved.

Peer pressure – Do you spend more money than you should when you're hanging out with friends? Even our best friends with the best intentions can be a bad influence, especially if they also have bad spending habits. When you can't afford to eat out, shop, or go on holiday, it's okay to decline their invitations. Feel free to be honest since they are likely to understand.

Or instead, suggest plans that won't make you spend more money. You can meet for coffee instead of brunch, explore new hiking trails instead of going to a concert or have a potluck dinner at home instead of eating at a restaurant.

You may not be having fancy dinners or expensive vacations, but you can still enjoy a great social life. On a minimalist budget, your social connections will not be sacrificed.

If you let your friends know you're trying to spend less, they can even help you on your journey, and some of them may want to follow in your footsteps. The most important thing is finding friends who will support you in achieving your financial goals.

Lifestyle – If you're used to a certain lifestyle, it can be difficult to give it up when faced with financial hardship. But if the overspending continues, you'll only end up in worse shape.

Your upbringing may have influenced your lifestyle choices. If you were brought up in a household where money was tight, you might feel the urge to spend more to compensate for the things you didn't get. Conversely, if you grew up in a family where money wasn't an issue, you'll want to maintain the lifestyle you grew up with. This can be financially detrimental if your source of money isn't the same as it used to be.

The easiest way to live within your means is to find cheaper alternatives. You may have to sacrifice a little bit of comfort, but it's better than losing a lot of comfort when your bank account gets in the red. It can be hard to give up certain luxuries, but no one's quality of life is compromised by this. Most luxury items are excessive, and you'll find that 'above average' brands, as opposed to high-end brands, are still extremely satisfying.

2. List your priorities

You need to categorize your monthly expenses into three main categories: wants, needs, and nice-to-have. Include expenses like car payments, rent, groceries, and utilities in the needs category. Items like new clothes or unnecessary gadgets should go under the wants category. Premium cable channels and entertainment should be listed in the nice-to-have category.

You should establish your goals based on this list. Consider casting the goals in positive terms, and not as things you have to live without. If you always spend $5 each day on fast food lunches, try cutting back to two fast-food lunches per week. Consider bringing lunch from home for the other three days. The extra $15 can be put towards one of your other goals. This will help in debt reduction and still satisfy your fast food cravings. This self-discipline can easily turn into a positive, lasting habit.

3. Learn to budget money

Without a plan, you won't stop erratic spending. If we fail to learn how much we take home and how much we spend, we will keep buying what we think we can afford. You will only realize after a month that you've wasted money when your bank account is empty and there's no taking your bad decisions back. To avoid this, learn to budget your money.

Start by adding up all your sources of income and then all your fixed expenses like debt repayments, rent, car payment, etc. The fixed expenses are easier to budget.

When that is done, list your variable expenses like gas, groceries, and entertainment and allocate funds to each category based on how much you've spent in the past.

Seeing how much you spend on clothing, entertainment, and other wants can help you save on what you don't need.

Try testing your budget. Track your spending for a month and compare that to what you've allocated in your budget. Make all necessary changes to your budget in the next month.

4.   Track your spending

The little purchases we make can add up to a huge amount. Without tracking them, your regrets will grow, too. Tracking expenses is the key to successful budgeting. It will keep you accountable for every dollar you spend. When you know where your money goes, it helps you make better choices in the future.

Many people start tracking bigger expenses, but it's crucial to pay attention to the smaller purchases as well. Those lunches out, morning lattes, lottery tickets, or magazine purchases can add up to more than you expect. In fact, you'll find that sometimes they can cost more than the bigger expenses, in the long run. This can affect your budget in significant ways.

5. Evaluate yourself honestly

Every month, compare your spending to what you intended to spend. It's a great time to hold yourself accountable. If you tend to overspend for certain categories, it's time to admit these are your problem areas. Stop making excuses for why you lost control and start reflecting on the real reason you've chosen to spend your money this way.

You need to be honest with yourself since the only person who suffers from this lack of discipline is you. Hold yourself to higher standards and know when it's time to get serious with yourself. Whatever the reason for your overspending is, there is most certainly an alternative that both fulfills the same need and is kinder to your wallet. Get creative and think about what these alternatives could be.

6. Spend wisely

Set aside money every month to cover all your required bills and expenses. Whether you set aside money on your computer or physically, make sure this is a habit you get used to. Resist all temptations to spend money on things other than the expenses.

Pay as many or as much of your bills as you can. Paying more towards your credit card bill, for instance, will reduce your owed balance quickly and save money on interest.

You can buy a "want" every two months so you don't feel deprived.

Resist the urge to get a new purse or the latest tech gadget that's all the rage. Instead, put these items on your birthday wish list or for any other holiday you celebrate. You can also set up a money jar for that item, and put change from your purse or pocket into it every evening. If you used a coupon at a store, put the amount you saved into the jar. Try selling unused items online or at a garage sale, and put the money you earned in the savings jar.

You'll be surprised by how easy money adds up without taking anything away from your monthly bills.

7. Pay off expenses

Make it easy to resist impulsive buying. Consider only carrying the cash you have budgeted for. And perhaps allow yourself a low-interest credit card only for when you really need it. Make sure to only use this credit card when it is absolutely necessary. Even a low-interest credit card can cause you significant debt if it is not used wisely.

Use unexpected income – tax refunds, birthday gifts, annual bonuses – to pay off a high-interest credit card or loan. Remind yourself that putting extra money towards your needs lets you make inroads into main expenses and allows you to pay them off sooner.

8. Reward yourself

Reward yourself when you've achieved significant goals. For example, after you've paid off a huge bill or successfully maintained self-discipline for a long period of time.

After renting movies for a whole month, reward yourself with a show at your local theatre. If you've successfully refrained from eating out on the weekends, reward yourself with one dinner out every month. You've saved money and made progress towards more disciplined spending habits. This is something worth celebrating – just make sure the celebration is within budget!

9. Define your motivations

It's crucial to understand what achieving financial security means for you. It could mean having the freedom to do whatever you want. Or perhaps it's travel, spending more time with family, or more time to write a novel.

Here are other examples to consider:

- Retiring early

- Having more money for hobbies

- Starting a non-profit organization

- Quitting your job and for a passion that offers lower pay or less stability

Whatever your true motivation is, it's crucial that you identify it and keep it in mind when you feel the nudge of spending urges. Try to figure out how else financial self-discipline can assist you in getting there and what the smaller steps to that destination are. Your motivations may also change over time. Make sure you can adapt to these changes.

10. Ditch the credit cards

When going to the grocery store or the mall, take the amount you think will be enough and leave the credit card at home. Unless you're sure you can pay it off soon, you shouldn't take credit cards with you at all.

This way you'll avoid impulse spending and the risk of getting into any debt. It's easy to make yourself promises in the heat of a shopping spree. Promises such as, "I'll just be more sensible the next couple of weeks and I can easily pay this off." But the next week, you end up saying the same thing, with no change t'

51

your behaviour. Eliminate the possibility of this happening and leave that credit card at home.

Having credit card information saved onto your online shopping profile can make it easy to spend impulsively. All it takes you is a click, and you'll be just a few shoes richer and a lot of dollars poorer.

When you delete these credit card numbers, you make it slightly less convenient to purchase needless items.

11. Set short-term financial goals

Setting attainable, short-term money goals is a perfect way to remain motivated as you change your spending habits. These goals will constantly remind you of the reasons why you are cutting back on expenses. It's important to focus on short-term goals because long-term goals can seem daunting. It'll take a long time before you achieve a long-term goal (hence the word long-term!) and you may feel you're not making progress. Watching your short-term goals get ticked off will motivate you to keep going. Break up your long-term goals into small, achievable steps.

And, it's also crucial to set specific goals. A goal like 'reduce spending on eating out' isn't going to work well because it isn't specific. You need quantifiable goals like 'I will reduce how much I spend on eating out from $150 to $75 a month.' These goals will give you a target to aim for.

'ome other short-term goals include:

Saving 10% of all paychecks in a different account

'ticking to a cash budget

'inging lunch to work for a whole month

'less of your goals, it's important you keep them simple,

le and out in the open to remind yourself daily.

)

Chapter 3 - Budgeting Strategies and Financial Plans

Budgeting and saving don't work for many people and for obvious reasons. Even when you have a well-laid out plan, spending on nonessentials is far too easy and straying from our goal is a common occurrence.

The basic concept behind budgeting is simple, but it's in the execution where people fail. To save money, all you need to do is not spend it. I mean, how hard can that be? This is what most of us tell ourselves when we try to establish money habits, but something always makes us lose focus.

There are a lot of budgeting strategies. Different strategies work for different people. You won't find a single budgeting strategy that works for everyone. With the right planning, diligence, and perseverance, it's possible to create and maintain an effective budget.

Before implementing a budgeting or financial plan, you need to know your reason for doing so. If you don't, chances are you won't want to create a budget. And even if you do create a budget, you aren't likely to stick to it if you don't know why it exists in the first place. Perhaps you have been reckless with your spending and you want to stop impulse purchases immediately. Or maybe you're on a debt repayment plan. Or perhaps you are good with your money, but you aren't making great headway on your long-term goals. Whatever the reason, start defining why you want to create a budget. This will keep you focused.

You will also have to figure out your priorities. Budgeting isn't all about math and numbers. It's about living the best way you can by improving your relationship with money. It's about finding out what's important to you and then changing your spending habits to meet your goals and values.

If you have money goals, write them down. Concentrate on the top priorities. The most important thing when concentrating on priorities is honesty. If your priorities are dishonest and don't reflect your personal values, you will be conflicted when making crucial decisions. You'll find it hard to stay motivated and on task. Be yourself when it comes to budgeting.

You also have to monitor your outflow. It's important to do this before and after creating a budget. That's because it can be impossible to know how much to allocate towards certain items without knowing how much you spend in a month. There are many apps and services that allow you to separate spending into categories.

You might discover something that will surprise you. You could find that while you feel you don't make enough, you make more than enough to cover all your expenses and still save for an emergency. Knowing where you stand will help you figure out where you want to be. If you learn that you make enough to save every month, you might want to see where you can cut back to start saving on emergency funds.

Now that you know what it takes to implement a budgeting strategy, we can take a deeper look.

4 powerful budgeting strategies to align your spending with your money-saving goals

There are a lot of ways you can approach budgeting. Some are very simple, while others are more complex and detailed. No method is better than the other. You just have to find a method that fits with your goals and personality. It's vital that you examine each one to determine which method suits you. The most common ones are:

1. 50/30/20 budgeting rule

With this rule, you spend 50% of your pay on needs like debts, insurance, groceries, utilities, and housing. 30% will go towards the expenses of your personal lifestyle. We can also label these as 'wants.' These expenses are the most likely to blow your budget out of order, so it's the most important to keep under control. It encompasses the things that you can do without, but make you happy nonetheless.

The remaining 20% of your income goes towards savings. This could be saved for retirement, working towards goals, or putting money into an investment. Use these on saving for a car, dream vacation, your children's college fund, and a house.

So, if you earn $5,000 every month, $2,500 should go towards your needs. $1,500 can be spent for your wants, and the remainder should be saved.

Some needs are obvious, but figuring out if something is a want or a need can be challenging. For example, work clothes would be a need, while trendy clothes to go out in would be classified as wants. You might need a monthly subscription service to back up your digital files to the cloud, but a music streaming service would be a want.

It is vital to categorize your needs and wants accordingly to stay on track.

2. Zero-sum budget

In this budget strategy, every dollar you make is assigned a job.

The amount of money you make minus your expenses should come to zero.

So, if your total income is $5,000 per month, find a place where that money will go. You should break up your budget into different categories. Consider car-related expenses, eating out, rent and utilities, personal items, groceries, debt, and insurance. If you've covered all your expenses and still have $500 left, you need to assign a task to those remaining dollars.

The value of this budgeting strategy is that it leaves nothing without a task. Every dollar is accounted for and used the way you want.

The best way you can approach a zero-sum budget is by writing it all down. Find out your anticipated income before the start of the month, then create a budget in which those dollars will go and make required adjustments as you progress.

3. Anti-budget

Contrary to what the name of this budget strategy suggests, it is still a spending plan of sorts. In this strategy, you won't have to worry about putting your expenses in specific categories. You pay as you go. The only catch is you must pay for your priorities first. You immediately pay all your necessary bills, such as rent and utilities, put a small portion in your retirement fund, and another portion in your savings account (we advise saving at least 20% of your income) and *voila!* You can spend the rest however you like. No tedious writing or flicking aimlessly through your bank statements.

This budgeting strategy is perfect for those who want to budget but have trouble starting. This requires consistency and an understanding of your priorities.

Define your priorities and make needs a priority before considering wants. Spend what you have on the necessities, then when all is paid, you can spend the rest on wants.

4.   Money flow budgeting

With this budgeting strategy, some trial and error is required.

When you have figured out how much you need each month to pay for all expenses, you can create a money flow. How does that work? The best way is to figure out what all your recurring expenses are and set up auto-pay for each of them. This includes fixed necessities such as utilities and rent. You will be paying off these expenses directly from your checking account. After money flows in on payday, your bills are paid as soon as they are due. You won't have to touch anything.

This budgeting strategy is best for those who want to forget about when bills are due. You must be comfortable with bill pay automation and of course, you must make the effort to arrange for this in the beginning.

When all the fixed expenses have been paid, take the rest of your income and make a budget. That means that you'll only monitor discretional and variable spending. This includes gas for the car, entertainment, groceries, etc. If you feel like it, you can also move this money into a separate debit card or bank account.

Better yet, if self-monitoring works well for you, you can use a credit card to manage variable expenses. Just make sure to pay the balance in full as the month ends.

You will still have to review your spending regularly and make changes if you feel you aren't making progress. The ideal outcome from this strategy is you'll do less monthly work, and be aware of everything that happens with your money. Even if most of the work is automated, it doesn't mean you get to stop paying attention.

One of these strategies will be suitable for you; you just need to discover which one it is. The approach you choose depends on how you work best, how much work you can put, and the details you want to insert into your budget. The most important thing is that you prioritize making a budget.

Making sure that budget strategy implementation is successful

1. Use your budget

A budget is useless if you don't use it. When you have identified a budget strategy that feels right for you, consider trying it out. Personal finance involves a lot of trial and error. Don't worry if you test out a strategy and it doesn't work. Just try another one instead. Your ideal budgeting strategy will depend on your lifestyle and personal taste. It's important that you find the one that works for you.

2. Update your budget regularly

You will always find room for improvement. Make it a habit to review and change your budget at regular intervals to get maximized benefits from your money. Budgeting takes time. Make a budget, live with it, and over time you'll notice what doesn't work, and you can adjust accordingly. Don't be discouraged if your lifestyle doesn't seem to fit the budget you've created. Feel free to tweak certain aspects until it works for you.

There are no rules you can apply to improve your budget.

Personal satisfaction should be your guideline. Are you satisfied with your monthly money management? Are you saving what you need? Are you able to adhere to the rules you've assigned? If you aren't, consider why.

3. Use existing habits to create new ones

Consider an established habit and use it to implement a new one. For example, let's say you always drink coffee every morning before heading to work. If you want to be better at checking how much money is left in your budget, connect these two habits in your daily routine. After drinking a cup of coffee, consider using a money app, or logging in to your bank account to check the balance. Checking your balance every time you drink a cup of coffee makes it easy to remember. As soon as you sit down with that cup of coffee, muscle memory will immediately have you examining your finances. Once this becomes part of your daily routine, you'll have total awareness of your financial standing at all times, making it less likely for you to make decisions that negatively impact it. The new habit of checking on your budget is easy to implement when you link it to a habit you are used to. Try it!

15 Easy steps to come up with a financial plan that lets you save more and earn more

A financial plan is a road map to guide you to a better future. It extends beyond just investing and budgeting. A good financial plan will help you navigate major financial milestones.

A financial plan acts as a set of principles or rules by which you live. The rules of your financial plan should help you in the grand scheme of your life. You need to have a flexible financial plan that allows you to adjust course when life gets tough. The core principles might stay the same, but finances can quickly change when you get married, buy a house, have kids, suffer from a disability or illness, get divorced, gear up for retirement or move across the country. A financial plan should act as a compass to get you back on track.

Your financial advisor might help you set up a plan, but most advisors are focused on product sales such as insurance, investments, and mortgages. Chances are they won't ask where you want to be in the next five years. Also, they might not truly understand your long and short-term money needs.

A better option is to work with a fee-only money advisor. They'll look at your financial health and come up with a plan to help you achieve your goals. The only problem is there are few fee-only advisors and a comprehensive plan might set you back thousands of dollars.

Another good idea is to create a basic financial plan. This process will make you think about money in ways you've never considered before.

Here are simple steps to help you create your financial plan:

1. Identify your goals

You must decide precisely what you want from your finances and which strategies will help you accomplish this.

Do you have children that are expected to attend college someday? If so, you need to save money to make that happen.

At what age do you intend to retire? Knowing this will help you figure out your goal and just how much time you have to achieve it.

Do you want to get out of debt completely? If so, add up all your debt, and determine how much you have to pay towards it each month to clear it in a particular amount of time.

You can also work with a financial planner to target the most realistic and worthwhile goals. Sometimes planners will tell their clients what they want to hear, but a good planner will tell clients what they need to hear.

Also, remember that paying your financial planner is a huge waste if you don't use their advice. It would be like going to a doctor and then failing to take the prescribed medication.

When you have established your goals, identify a solid plan.

2. Setting up a budget

All financial planning requires you to spend less money than you make. Whether your goal is to retire early or pay off your mortgage, you need extra money to make such a goal a reality. That's why you need a budget. You will find that many people skip this step, which is why they never achieve any meaningful financial goals.

A lot of people think that budgets add stress, but most of the time, it does the opposite.

3. Cutting expenses

Identify the necessary expenses in your budget. These are what you must pay no matter what. Then identify the expenses that are important but that you could live without. These are necessary, can be cut to some degree.

Identify the discretionary expenses. These may be desirable, but they are not necessary. You can completely eliminate these expenses without affecting your survival.

When you have all your expenses in proper categories, it's time to make reductions. Reduce important expenses and eliminate some discretionary expenses.

4. Eliminate debt

It doesn't make sense to invest and save money when you are paying a lot of interest on the debt you owe.

Getting out of debt requires discipline, but it's possible. If you're in a lot of debt, you must drastically cut spending and increase earnings to pay it off quickly. Include all your debt except the first mortgage on your home.

When you are out of debt, set up systems that will prevent you from going back into debt. This includes setting aside money for big purchases and carrying the right health insurance so you don't take on sudden medical debt.

5. Build an emergency fund

When you are out of debt, consider building an emergency fund that can cater to your expenses for six months. This cushion will allow you to leave your investments alone during hard times. This should only be used for real emergencies like job loss, to protect retirement savings and investments.

If you must dip into the emergency fund, focus on returning the money as soon as possible. If you have an unstable job, you should consider saving up to cater for expenses for one year should an emergency arise.

If you are creating a financial plan while still paying off debt, set up a smaller emergency fund of about $1,500 or a month's income to help you cover unexpected expenses. This will ensure you get out of debt without adding more debt.

6. Determine your net worth

Figure out where you are before thinking about where you want to be. Create a net worth statement to get an idea of your financial situation.

Sum up all your assets and subtract the liabilities. What remains is your net worth. Play around with reduced versions of your current expenses. Seeing the final amount just might motivate you to make cut those expenses for real!

7. Check your cash flow

If you want a strong financial plan, you should understand how much you save and spend. You can use an app or spreadsheet to track the money that comes in from interest, wages, and government benefits, and the money that goes out for debt payments, rent, and utility bills.

Fill your monthly expenses in a column and the annual expenses in a different column. Add up the expenses in both columns and then subtract them from the total net income on a yearly and monthly basis. You will get your cash flow surplus or deficit.

Tracking your cash flow will give you a sense of confidence and control which makes it easier to implement financial changes.

8. Match your goals to your spending

Since you have identified your goals and determined the cash flow, it's time to compare your goals to your spending. How well do your spending habits mesh with your goals? If you continue with the spending habits that you have now, will you ever reach your goals? If so, how long will it take?

If there's a cash flow deficit, it means you won't meet your goal, so you'll have to reduce certain expenses to ensure there's money left over. If there is a cash surplus, then you can begin allocating money to meet your goals. Make sure that you put your priorities before your non-essentials.

9. Review your insurance coverage

Many employer plans provide minimal life insurance coverage. Basic calculations will help you determine if it covers enough. You should ensure that your life insurance is enough to pay off the debts you owe. Also, it should cover ten times your income when you have kids below the age of 10, and five times your income if you have kids above 10.

10. Reduce taxes

Most families have a straightforward tax plan and chances are that you already take advantage of the best tax shelters when owning a home or when you contribute to your TFSA, RRSP, and RESP.

But if you are self-employed and rely on rental income, commission income, or significant investment income, you can hire an accountant to assist you on income tax planning.

11. Create an investment policy

A good financial plan should have an investment policy statement that gives advice on how your portfolio should be invested.

When you write down your investment policy on paper, it will help you stay on track with investments when markets become volatile.

You can create a simple policy. For example, stating that you should invest in low cost, widely diversified ETFs or index funds that will be rebalanced annually to maintain 25% Canadian bonds, 25% US equities, 25% Canadian equities, and 25% international equities. The new money will be added to the lowest valued funds for you to buy low.

12. Create a will and keep it updated

Every adult with assets, children and a spouse should have a will. You need an accurate and up-to-date will so that your assets can be distributed the way you want after you have gone.

Financial planning doesn't end when you die. You should make provisions for what might happen to your property when you are gone. If you don't have a will, chances are the survivors will end up in court battling for your assets. Your assets might even end up disappearing.

Make some time and meet with a trusted attorney to come up with a will that distributes your assets according to your wishes.

Create one now and you can make adjustments in the future if your financial situation changes. All that's important is that actions are taken to prevent your assets from being the subject of conflict.

13. Save for retirement

Perhaps you've been saving for retirement, even if it's just a small amount every month. As soon as you get out of debt, your cash flow will increase, allowing you to save more money for retirement.

If you haven't started saving yet, start with an amount that won't hurt your financial situation. Your goal should be to increase your contribution every year.

You can achieve this by directing your future pay increase into the contribution. You can also increase it by redirecting debt payments once you've paid off debt. If you have a strong financial situation, you'll feel confident contributing a huge amount to your retirement plan, like bonus checks and income tax refunds.

14. Save for other goals

There are a lot of other reasons to save money. Saving for a future college education or a new car are perfect examples.

The reason to save for these other goals is so that more money is available for other expenses and so you can avoid getting into debt to pay for them.

It is no use to work hard to get out of debt, only to fall back into it when faced with a big expense.

Many people get stuck in a debt cycle they can never seem to recover from. That's why a good financial plan should include a prevention strategy. This involves saving money for things that will happen in the future.

You can set up an automatic weekly deposit into your savings account. You can save $150 per week instead of $500 per month. Smaller amounts may be more realistic than larger amounts.

15. Invest and diversify

When you have maxed out the eligibility on your retirement accounts, you can use other tools like annuities, mutual funds, or real estate to increase your investment portfolio.

You should diversify the types of investments you make. If you are careful and consistent with your investments, there will be a point where the investments make more money that you do. This is a great thing to have in place when you retire, especially since this is passive income.

When you are closer to retiring, you might want to change the way you invest. Make safer investments that won't be affected by market changes. This ensures that you have the money you need even if the economy crashes. When you are young, you have enough time for the market to recover. You can get a financial advisor if you need help with this.

Chapter 4 - Get out of debt

<u>A short message from the Author:</u>

Hey! Sorry to interrupt. I just wanted to check in and ask if you're enjoying the Minimalist Budget audiobook? I'd love to hear your thoughts!

Many readers and listeners don't know how hard reviews actually are to come by, and how much they help an author.

So I would be incredibly thankful if you could take just 60 seconds to leave a quick review on Audible, even if it's just a sentence or two!

And don't worry, it won't interrupt this audiobook.

To do so, just click the 3 dots in the top right corner of your screen inside of your Audible app and hit the "Rate and Review" button.

This will take you to the "rate and review" page where you can enter your star rating and then write a sentence or two about the audiobook.

It's that simple!

I look forward to reading your review. Leave me a little message as I personally read every review!

Now I'll walk you through the process as you do it.

Just unlock your phone, click the 3 dots in the top right corner of your screen and hit the "Rate and Review" button.

Enter your star rating and that's it! That's all you need to do.

I'll give you another 10 seconds just to finish sharing your thoughts.

----- Wait 10 seconds -----

Thank you so much for taking the time to leave a short review on Audible.

I am very appreciative as your review truly makes a difference for me.

Now back to your scheduled programming.

Many people have plans to pay off debt and most of them fail because they haven't identified their true motivation. You may start out fully motivated to repay all debt, but it's easy to become discouraged after making it past the initial stages.

If you want to keep your momentum, you need to continually remind yourself of the reasons you need to get out of debt. How will paying off your debt benefit you? What can't you do now that you can when you're debt-free?

If you haven't identified your true motivation, do so now. Your motivation is the reward you're striding towards. Defining it will make you realize just how much you want it, and how hard you're willing to work to achieve it.

Getting out of debt increases your financial security. It is a serious threat to financial security. The amount you spend on debt payments could have been saved for an emergency, retirement, or for your child's college fund. Being debt-free allows you to be financially secure.

Debt also prevents you from saving money for things you enjoy. Unfortunately, this is why people get deeper into debt. They can't afford the things they love so they make payments on credit until they can't borrow any more. Paying off all debt frees you from this vicious cycle and allows you to spend your income on what you enjoy.

Debt can also lead to more stress as you worry about covering debt payments as well as other expenses. A little stress occasionally isn't harmful, but stress all the time can lead to serious health issues like migraines and heart attacks. Becoming debt free can save your life.

What's unfortunate about debt is the more people you owe, the more bills you must keep up with. When you are debt free, you have fewer bills every month. You'll only have to worry about basic expenses like cell phone service, insurance, and utilities.

A debt-free person has a higher credit score. A huge debt, like credit card debt, will have a negative impact on your credit score.

A debt-free person also teaches their children good money habits by example. If you want your kids to stay away from debt, show them the importance of being debt-free and how to live a debt-free life.

Find out what causes debt

Have you ever considered the reason you're in a debt? Have you ever scrutinized these reasons? We all know that debt can lead us to disastrous consequences in our lives. Sometimes it consumes our assets, hurts our relationships, and brings about intense mental stress.

Many people have fallen deep into the black hole of financial debt. While we may know of the obvious reasons why, there are other factors that lead to debt accumulation.

Most people have spent their adult life in debt and there is nothing fun about it, but it doesn't have to define you.

Even though there are effective debt elimination programs like debt settlement and consolidation, we must be aware of the things that lead us to make great financial errors so that we can avoid them.

1. Failing to use money wisely

The first mistake that gets us into debt is overspending. Many people have gotten into financial trouble because they spent more than they could afford. This usually happens when you fail to set up a budget or create one and fail to stick to it.

If you spend more than you earn, you must learn how to cut your expenses. And once you've cut your expenses, it's time to figure out how you can earn more money.

Another way that people fail to use their money wisely is by not getting insurance. This has made many individuals and businesses fall into huge debt. When you have an adequate insurance cover, especially health insurance, you will stay afloat during an emergency.

The same happens to small businesses. If a small business fails to take out general liability insurance or other insurance covers, they could face significant financial loss if an accident occurs or if they are sued. Business insurance is crucial to all businesses for basic protection.

Some people also fail to save for an emergency fund, so they get into huge debt when an emergency strikes. Even saving a small amount of money can make a big difference. Without an emergency fund, it can be hard to recover from an emergency. You'll have to use your savings or pay with credit. This can lead to a large accumulation of debt.

Some people get into a habit of gambling and end up losing a lot of money. Many view gambling as the best kind of entertainment, but it's just a guaranteed way of giving gambling companies your money. As loans are readily available these days, people are addicted to the idea of winning the lottery and becoming rich. Gambling can lead someone to throw their future away as they try to recover the money they have lost.

2. Life uncertainty

Sometimes things happen in our life that we don't expect and they end up causing financial problems. For instance, medical surgeries can be expensive. Medical costs and expenses can sometimes lead people into debt. If someone has gone through major medical surgery, chances are their insurance will not cover the full cost. Sometimes they may not be insured at all. When this happens, they could easily accumulate huge debt. It can be hard to avoid the massive cost of the procedure, but you can still find great hospitals that charge lower than the rest. You don't have to go to a specific hospital unless your insurance requires it.

Another uncertainty is inflation. Most people don't realize how much the cost of living has gone up. Between gas, food, and housing, and other expenses, most people won't receive a pay rise to offset these increases. If they can't cut back on spending, it might lead to more debt. If you leave your money in a regular savings account, your savings might be stripped due to inflation.

Another reason why people get into debt is a change of income. People will struggle to pay bills, and quickly suck up savings or turn to credit cards.

You might also move to a different house and the council tax band may become high. Perhaps your landlord increases your rent. The interest rate on a mortgage could also go up. How will you cope with these changes? This can easily send a person into debt.

Divorce can also present a strain on personal expenses. There are laws that govern what needs to be done with money during a divorce settlement. If one party demands too much, the other one might have to go into debt to pay for an attorney as well as what the other partner wants as part of the settlement.

4. Identity theft

Identity theft occurs when a criminal illegally opens up an account in your name and then runs up a huge amount of debt. The victim will be left with all the debt that someone else accumulated and they must pay for it. Identity theft cases have been on the rise and it could happen to anyone. To prevent such a disaster from happening to you, make sure that you keep all personal information as safe as possible. This includes your social security number and bank account numbers. Do not give this information to anyone unless you are 100% certain you can trust them. Bank officials usually have other ways of confirming your identity if they need to do so over the phone, so never be forthcoming with a caller who claims to be from your bank. In addition to these precautions, make sure to never leave important mail out in plain sight, where others can easily take hold of them.

5. Lack of financial knowledge

A lot of people don't have the financial experience or education required to make wise financial decisions. They may end up relying on credit cards or getting high-interest loans because they don't know what the best thing to do is. They may also fall for the tricks of many financial institutions. Often credit cards will be offered with seemingly fantastic benefits, and unbeknownst to the financially unaware target, the card will come with a myriad of hidden fees and high-interest. To avoid this, always go through the fine print and make sure you understand what it means.

Also, poor budgeting leads to debt. A person with good financial knowledge knows how important a monthly budget is. Without a good budget, you won't be able to track where your money goes. If you keep track of spending for a whole month, you will see exactly where your money goes and what you need to cut. This is where you can learn about unnecessary expenses. Without this, you can easily overspend and accumulate debt.

6. Expanding families

Many married and single people may feel they have a lot of extra money, but once they decide to have kids, that can change. Your expenses shoot up sharply with each child you have, sometimes more than people even expect. Sometimes families may have to forego one income, which can hurt their finances. If you don't have a kid, then you might not understand how day-care services can cost a lot, but it's something you should always keep in mind, if you're thinking of having a child. You'd be surprised by the amount of money that childcare costs. Make sure to consider all the expenses before you make this huge decision.

7. Taxes and high-interest charges

For most people, federal taxes have been flat for years, but state, produce, and local taxes have continued to increase. This means the average person has less spending money. There are taxes everywhere and the more money we make, the more we're taxed.

Many credit card accounts have interest rates that exceed 20%. This can make it impossible to repay debt. Many have fallen deep into debt because of credit cards.

8. Poor investments

People may have good intentions when they start investing but sometimes these investments turn out to be terrible choices and they end up losing money. This is why it's important to have a decent understanding on what you're investing in. Many people make the mistake of investing in things they barely comprehend.

Sometimes investing can be complicated, but it doesn't have to be. You need to be careful when investing or else you could incur major losses that are difficult to recover from. Consider keeping your investments simple or only making big choices when you have a complete understanding or the guidance of an expert.

9. Burying one's head in the sand

Failing to open emails on your doormat, avoiding phone calls from your creditors and ignoring financial issues will see you get into debt quickly.

Perhaps you don't have enough time to deal with your finances or you think that not opening your mail will make the situation go away. Both assumptions are completely wrong. When you fail to deal with the situation, things will just get worse and accumulate. If you are unable to pay a household bill, then call them. Explain to them why you can't pay and discuss plans. Stare that number in the face and come up with a plan for getting it settled.

Ignoring one bill might turn it into debt. Ignoring two bills might turn it into worse debt with added interest charges. You may even start seeing letters from a solicitor or a debt management company. They will start chasing these payments and this will affect your credit score. Fees will soon come as well. You may be taken to court and given a CCJ. Enforcement agents will turn up unannounced and knock on your door. To avoid this, pick up those calls and stop avoiding those letters.

10. Comparing yourself to others

Spending money because you think you need the same things as others will soon get you into debt. This is especially true if you cannot afford these things. Most people in society want something their neighbors have, but even if they acquire whatever it is they desire, they'll soon find that they hunger for something else. Desire can become a bottomless pit and unfortunately your money source is far from bottomless. Fashion changes every season and the media pushes products to manufacture desires. It doesn't matter what others are doing. Quit comparisons now. The liberation you'll feel will go beyond anything money can buy.

11 practical techniques to help you get out of debt - regardless of the amount

No matter what you are going through, whether you borrowed a loan or maxed out your credit card, it's your obligation to pay it back. Even if you've faced a life-changing experience like an accident, job loss, or an increase in expenses after having a child, debt will not suddenly decide to be kind.

Overspending can happen at any time of the year. Most people try to get out of debt, but life gets tougher and some end up giving up. This shouldn't be the case for you. There are a lot of people who get out of debt every day. Most people do it in a short amount of time.

If you've started a journey towards financial freedom, you should have a plan for how to handle debt. You may be wondering what the point is if you'll be financially free.

Think of that big project you're planning for. Perhaps it's a home renovation, a school or work assignment, or sorting the garage. Some projects are so daunting that we end up putting them off for a while. A lot of people find it impossible to pay off debt because they deal with them in this manner.

They put off answering the phone, opening the mail, or making any kind of reparation because it seems too big a task. They act as if not looking at the problem will make it disappear.

As tempting as it can be to give into stagnation, the best way to tackle a huge project is to break up tasks into smaller achievable steps. This same rule applies to getting out of debt. Here are the techniques that will help you:

1. Pay off more than the minimum

If you have a credit card balance of about $15,000, and you pay a 15% APR, and make a minimum monthly payment of $600, it will take about 13 years to pay it off. That's only if you don't borrow more money in the meantime. This can be a huge challenge.

Whether you have a personal loan, credit card debt, or student loans, the best way to get out of debt soon is to pay more than the minimum monthly payment. When you do so, you'll save on interest while you repay the loan. It will help you pay off the debt sooner. To avoid headaches, ensure that your loan doesn't charge you prepayment penalties before getting started.

If you need help, there are many mobile and online repayment tools that will help you. They will help you track and chart your progress as you try to clear the balances.

2. Use excess cash to pay off debt

Whenever extra money fall into your lap, use it to speed up the debt repayment process. Some good examples of this unexpected money include an inheritance, profits from selling a car, a tax refund, and winnings from a bet. The more money you put towards debt repayment, the faster it will be cleared. Debt repayment doesn't have to take forever. Use the money you get from your annual raise or work bonus to speed things up.

Any time you get an unusual source of income, divert the money and use it wisely. You can even use the money to clear the smallest balance so that you can concentrate on the largest balance. Resist the tendency to see excess cash as money that you can spend on absolutely anything. As soon as you see excess money in your account, imagine how wonderful it will feel to deduct that excess amount from your debt instead. By paying off debt, you're indirectly making that surplus amount even higher! How? Cause paying off debt reduces your interest rate very slightly. You may regret buying another pair of shoes that looks exactly like another pair you own, but no one regrets paying off their debt.

3.   Try the debt snowball method

Consider trying the debt snowball method to build momentum and speed up the debt repayment process.

The first step involves listing all your debts and arranging them from the smallest to largest. Whenever you have excess funds, start by repaying the smallest amount on the list. Consider making minimum payments on the larger loans. When the smallest balance has been paid off, start using the excess funds to repay the next smallest debt until you clear that one and so on.

As time goes by, you'll clear the smaller balances, and more money will be available to clear the larger loans. Clearing the smaller balances first means you'll see less loans on your list much sooner.

4.   Get a part-time job

Eliminating debt with the snowball method might speed up the repayment process, but making more money can speed up the process even more.

Most people have a skill or a talent they can monetize. It could be babysitting, cleaning houses, mowing yards, or becoming a virtual assistant. If no talent comes to mind, check sites like Craigslist for one-time gigs that you can do on the weekends or evenings to make some extra cash.

Look for a part-time job in your area with a local retailer who might need seasonal workers to assist when the stores are busy. These part-time jobs can help you make enough money to get out of debt.

There are other seasonal jobs you can get. During springtime, there are a lot of farm and greenhouse jobs that can benefit you.

During the summer, you can try being a tour operator, landscaper or lifeguard. During the fall, there are seasonal jobs at pumpkin patches, haunted house attractions, and for fall harvest.

No matter the time of year, you will always find a temporary job to help with finances. All it takes is a little extra motivation and some creativity.

5. Make debt repayments as often as you can

This strategy pays off when it comes to taking care of your mortgage. When you make monthly payments, you will end up paying more interest and miss out on taking advantage of time.

Time will keep moving regardless of how you make your payments, so the easiest and least painful strategy to pay your mortgage loans is to accelerate payments

Change your monthly payment frequency to semi-monthly, weekly or bi-weekly. This will depend on how often you get a paycheck. This change will save you money and time. The best strategy to tackle a big project is to break it into smaller steps.

Making frequent payments is also a perfect strategy to pay off your credit card debt. The more often you make payments, even if it's just with extra money, the less likely you are to waste it on something you won't need. If you want to get out of debt, find ways to make payments as often as you can.

6. Create and live with a bare-bones budget

If you want to get out of debt quickly, you should cut down on expenses as much as possible. You can use a bare-bones budget to help you with this. This strategy involves getting expenses as low as possible and living a simple life for as long as you can.

A bare-bones budget is different for everyone, but it should aim to eliminate all extra expenses like cable television, eating out, or other unnecessary spending.

You should remember that a bare-bones budget is meant to be used temporarily. When you are out of debt, or when you are closer to your goal, you can start adding these extras back into your budget.

Having a budget that tracks your income and expenses is important when it comes to getting out of debt in a short time. The budget will help you gauge your financial status so you can get closer to your goals.

A budget will show you whether you have surplus money, or if you have a deficit.

7. Try the laddering method

The laddering method involves listing all your debts, starting with debt that has the highest interest rate and ending with low-interest debt.

This method will save you a significant amount of time with continued use. You will be saving the money you would have used for interest when you clear debt with the highest interest. When you choose this strategy, you need to stick with it. Every month, put as much money as you can towards the debt with the highest interest rate, while still paying the required minimums on other cards. When the debt is paid off, divert the excess funds to the second debt with the second highest interest rate and so on. It is important not to close the account when you have paid off the balance. It will damage your credit. Just let the account sit without funds for a while.

If you have small debts that you can easily pay off, then do so. It will bring you tangible progress to get you started. When you have done that, start tackling the card with the highest interest rate.

8. Sell the things you don't need

If you are looking for a way to get some quick cash, consider selling some of your belongings. Most people have a lot of things in their homes that they don't need. These can range from outgrown clothes to finished books. Chances are there is a heap of stuff you've forgotten about that you'll likely never use again. Take a look around your home and rid yourself of the stuff that you forgot existed. Why not sell those items and use the money for something more worthwhile?

If you live in an area that permits an old-fashioned garage sale, then perhaps that will do. It is the easiest and cheapest way to unload unwanted belongings and make money. If that's not an option, consider selling them through an online reseller, consignment shop, or a Facebook yard sale group.

9. Avoid impulse spending

If saving extra money is what's holding you back, consider tracking your expenses for some weeks to know where your money goes. You might be surprised about your spending habits. Most people don't realize how quickly little expenses can add up. Perhaps you love grabbing a newspaper, buying coffee daily, getting takeout instead of making dinner. These can be categorized as impulse buys if they are purchases that seem to happen automatically. You are so sure you can afford this that you don't even think about it. Learn to make each buy intentional and resist the urge to buy impulsively. These spending habits will prevent you from saving enough money to clear your debt.

There are also other habits that cannot be noticed easily, for example, subscriptions to television channels that you never watch, downloading apps and ringtones, buying toys and gifts at a grocery store because it's convenient.

You can get almost everything you want any time at a local supercentre grocery store. If you want to get out of debt, make sure you avoid impulse purchases.

10. Ask for lower interest rates on credit cards and negotiate other bills

If credit card interest rates are high, it can be impossible to make headway on your balance. Consider calling your card issuer and negotiate. You may not know this, but asking for lower interest rates happens a lot. If you have a good history of paying your bills on time, chances are that you'll get a lower interest rate.

Other than credit cards, other bills can be negotiated down or eliminated. Remember the worst answer you can get is no. The less you pay for fixed expenses, the more money you get for debt payment.

If you are not the negotiating type, consider using apps that will review your purchase history. They'll find repeated fees and forgotten subscriptions you might want to cut from your budget.

11.   Consider balance transfers

If a credit card company won't change their interest rates, perhaps it's a good idea to consider a balance transfer. There are a lot of balance transfer offers and you can secure a 0% APR for 15 months. However, you might have to pay a balance transfer fee of about 3% for the privilege.

Some cards don't charge a balance transfer fee for the first two months. They also offer a 0% introductory APR on purchases and balance transfers for the first 15 months.

If you have a credit card balance you can feasibly pay off during the time frame, transferring the balance to a card with 0% introductory APR could save you some money on interest while helping you pay down your debt faster.

It can be easy to continue living in debt if you have never faced the reality of the situation you are in. But when disaster hits, you'll gain a painfully new outlook quickly. One can also get sick of living a paycheck-to-paycheck lifestyle, and consider other ways to make ends meet.

No matter the type of debt you are in – whether it's from car loans, student loans, or another type of debt – it's crucial to know you can get out of it. It might not happen in a day, but a debt-free future can be achieved when one create a plan. You will have to stick to the plan for success.

No matter the plan you have, these strategies can help you get out of debt sooner than you thought. The faster you get out of debt, the quicker you can start living a life you've always wanted.

Chapter 5 - Make more with less

A short message from the Author:

Hey! We've made it to the final chapter of the audiobook and I hope you've enjoyed it so far.

If you have not done so yet, I would be incredibly thankful if you could take just a minute to leave a quick review on Audible, even if it's just a sentence or two!

Many readers and listeners don't know how hard reviews actually are to come by, and how much they help an author.

To do so, just click the 3 dots in the top right corner of your screen inside of your Audible app and hit the "Rate and Review" button.

Then you'll be taken to the "rate and review" page where you can enter your star rating and then write a sentence or two.

It's that simple!

I look forward to reading your review as I personally read every single one.

I am very appreciative as your review truly makes a difference for me.

Now back to your scheduled programming.

Whether you have some reserve in the tank or are living paycheck to paycheck, you're likely considering how to increase your income. How can you earn more money without losing more time in your day?

It's hard to persist when you have financial problems, but what other options do you have? At the end of the day, this comes down to how you use the money you have and your money mindset. There are a lot of benefits to positive thinking, but that alone isn't enough to help you increase your income.

You must act. That's what it takes. But before you act, you need to know what to do. How will you increase your income so you have enough money at the end of the month? First, you will have to learn how to maximize the use of your income, save enough money, and how to invest and build your personal assets.

Learn how to maximize the use of your income

If you find some extra money in your budget, chances are that you'll use it. While it might seem fun to use it on things you have always wanted, that's not a smart thing to do. The wisest thing to do is spend money on whatever can help you and your family.

You don't have to put all your money in a savings account. While it's good to save some money for difficult times, there are a lot of ways to maximize how you use your income. Although these purchases may not be fun to you, they can help you invest in your future. These wise ways to spend your money will help you live a happy life knowing you're using your money responsibly.

1. Pay off debt

If you want even more money to spend, pay off your debt. It is one of the smartest ways to spend your money. For instance, if you owe $2000 on a credit card and normally send the creditor $250 per month, why not use the tax return to pay off your debt? Then you'll have an extra $250 every month. While you may have plans for that money, clearing up $250 per month can make a huge difference in your budget.

2. Buy insurance

Insurance is one of those things we hope we never need, but if we have it when we need it, it can make a huge difference. You need to invest in a plan that will help you. For instance, having a health insurance plan helps to ensure that you always get affordable costs, should you get sick. This also applies to life insurance, home insurance, and auto insurance. When you have a good insurance plan, you are better equipped to handle life's unexpected events. When we put our income towards insurance, we make sure we have all we need in the future, should certain events occur.

3. Invest in a retirement plan

Another excellent way to maximize your income is by investing in a retirement plan. This will help you if you don't want to spend the rest of your life working. Consider investing in your future. If offered, consider having a 401(k) at work, and match what your employer contributes. If you want to take a step further, you can open an IRA. You will be required to invest each year, and the amount you pay will depend on your age.

4. Do home improvements

You don't want to buy a new window or roof until you must. However, investing in home improvements can increase your home's value. In some cases, these improvements can lower your electricity expenses. For instance, buying a new refrigerator can significantly reduce your electricity bill. Home improvements can increase the resale value of your home and turn it into an investment instead of a huge expense. Before doing home improvements, make sure to ask an expert what changes will raise the value of your home the most. Some improvements will be worth more than others.

5. Invest in education

It's always a good idea to invest your money in education. You can take a class to learn a new skill for a job, learn a new hobby, or start a new career or degree to help you get a promotion. A small price now could bring bigger earnings in, down the road.

Whatever your reasons are for investing in education, taking classes can be beneficial. Many will agree it's worth the time and money. In some instances, your employer might even reimburse you for the classes you take. Remember to check with your company first. You could also get tax benefits.

6. Attend a conference

Attending a conference is a great investment. You'll get the latest information about your area of expertise to help you be more successful at what you do. You can meet a lot of people and build a great network. If you are self-employed, it's a perfect way to let potential clients know about your services. You'll have access to a bigger pool of likely customers and this will increase your cash inflow.

Can you live on half your income and save the rest? Probably.

How soon could you achieve financial independence, if you could live on half of what you earn and invest the rest?

Probably within six years, and almost certainly less than ten years.

You should note that retirement and financial independence are not just about how much you earn. It's about how much of your expenses you can pay off with the income from your investments.

You can speed up that process in two ways: increase investments and lower your expenses. Well, the good news is that these two goals can be achieved with the same process. It involves living on a percentage of your income and investing the rest to get more passive income.

Consider this challenge: assume that you can live on half your income and eliminate disbelief. What financial moves would you need to get there?

1. Make two-week's pay your new budget

When creating your monthly budget, you usually take four week's income into account. Occasionally you will get a bonus paycheck, but normally you'll receive paychecks for four weeks.

If you are normally paid biweekly, it means you receive two paychecks in a month. Your challenge would be how you can live on one pay

check. That's after taxes. That's your new budget.

Does it seem impossible? Well, what would happen if you lose your job tomorrow, spent the next six months without a job, and eventually got a job earning about half your income? Would you be out on the street? Would you starve?

No, you'd have to pay down your expenses and move on. That means its 100% possible to live on half your income. All you have to do is make some lifestyle changes.

Your new budget should only be one paycheck's worth of income. Start by writing your fixed monthly expenses. That includes fixed utility bills, car payment, housing, and other expenses. Then write down your variable expenses like gas for your car, usage-based bills, groceries, and others. And finally, write down semi-annual and annual recurring expenses, such as holiday gifts, insurance, accountant costs, etc.

When you have all that, just cut down unnecessary expenses to fit your new budget.

2.   Eliminate or reduce housing costs

For most people, housing is the largest expense, and it's the first expense that you should scrutinize. Lucky for you, there is a way you can do this without moving to a less desirable home.

This involves getting a small multi-unit property, moving into one of the units, and leasing out the remaining units. The renters will contribute to the housing costs by paying you rent directly.

If you don't want to purchase a new home or move, there are still some options for you. You can segment part of your property as an income suite and then lease it out. You can sign a long-term lease agreement.

Or perhaps you can leave the whole separate income suite, and get a housemate. Housemates come with amazing advantages beyond paying rent. They help with house chores, cook meals, pay utility bills, and they can even become close friends.

If none of this sounds doable, then why not consider moving to a smaller home? A minimalist lifestyle will downsize your possessions so you may need less space than you did before. Perhaps even consider moving to a slightly less popular neighbourhood. All of these factors can reduce your rent significantly, and it doesn't necessarily mean your home is any less comfortable or attractive.

3. Learn to cook

Eating out or paying someone to cook for you can create huge expenses. They are budget killers and let's face it, they're not necessary.

Why don't you learn to cook? With time, you'll get better at it and you may even learn to enjoy it.

Anyone can learn to cook, and once you get over the initial awkwardness, you can learn to complete a three-course meal that beats anything at an overpriced restaurant. It will cost significantly lower prices to cook, and you can make extra food for the next day.

Also, when you cook for yourself, you'll end up cooking healthier meals than anything you'll find at a restaurant. You can pick low-carb or low-fat dishes and ingredients. Restaurants only prioritize taste, meaning excessive salt is often used.

4. Move your social life away from shopping

Where do you normally meet your friends? Bars? Movie theatres? Restaurants?

Since you can now cook, you can invite them over for dinner. You can also take cooler drinks somewhere with an amazing view instead of the bar. Instead of overpaying to get a movie ticket, plan a movie night at your or your friend's home. These days, movies can be rented online for a few dollars, and if you're tech savvy, they can even be streamed for free.

You could spend $100 eating out at a restaurant with friends, or you could spend $20 getting together for a bonfire or a picnic at the beach. Consider other options as well, such as a home wine-tasting or a backyard BBQ.

All it takes is a little more creativity and planning, but it will help you save an enormous amount of money without losing out on fun with friends.

5. Earn more money

If you are struggling to make ends meet with a two-week income, look for other ways to make more money. There are a lot of ways you can deal with this. You could negotiate for a pay rise at your workplace, or you could look for a new job that pays better. Find anything that can make you a more valuable employee and do it. If that's not possible, look for a part-time job to earn extra money.

What skills do you have that others need? Can you build websites on WordPress? Are you good at photography, and willing to work weddings for some weekend evenings every month? Do you have home improvement experience?

We all have skills, and everyone can learn to develop them. There are many ways to earn money, but it requires initiative on your part.

6. Automatically transfer half of your income

You will always be tempted to use money in your operating or checking account.

You can set up an automatic transfer from your account to an investment or savings account. You should do this transfer the same day you are paid.

In the beginning, you can use half of your income to pay off your debts. When all the debts are paid off, your budget will be very easy to deal with. With no debts, you can begin investing in high-yield investments that pay you. You will soon start rising, and you will be in a fantastic cycle where your income keeps on increasing.

That cycle will only take off if you keep expenses low. Most people only go out to spend when they get more money. They want a new car, fancy dinners out, a new house, and new clothes. That's what they call lifestyle inflation, and it's an enemy of financial independence.

7. Eliminate one money-draining habit

Alright, so maybe you're not ready to give up your entire lifestyle yet. In that case, start with one hobby or habit that costs you money every month. If you can't think of anything, check your most recent bank statement and highlight the deductions that went to wants, not needs. If you go to the movies a couple of times every month, stop going and stream your movies instead. If you enjoy purchasing stuff on Amazon every few weeks, stop doing it and replace it with a cheaper alternative like going to the library every few weeks. Once you've successfully eliminated a habit, you can continue you with your other money-wasting habits.

8. Push your mental boundaries

Our biggest limitations are our minds. Begin by working backward with your budget, cut your expenses down and boost your income. With discipline and creativity, it's possible to live on half your income. All it takes is your determination and perseverance.

Get the information you need to start investing

Do you want to invest but have no idea where to start? The first step to investing is the most important. If you invest wisely, it can lead to financial independence and passive income.

If you want to start investing, you need to have the right information so you avoid wasting your money on poor investments. So, what information should you have to get started? Here is what you need to know to ensure your investment is a success:

1. Decide on the type of assets you want to own

Investing is about putting money in something today and getting more money out of it in the future. Usually, you can achieve that by acquiring productive assets. For instance, if you buy an apartment building, you will own the property and the cash that it produces through rent.

Each productive asset has unique characteristics as well as pros and cons. Here are some of the potential investments you might consider:

Business equity – Owning equity in a business enables you to share a profit or loss generated by the company. Whether you want to own that equity by buying shares of a publicly traded business or acquiring a small business outright, business equities are the most rewarding asset class.

Fixed income securities - When you decide to invest in

fixed income security, you are lending money to a bond issuer. In exchange, you will get an interest income. You can do so in many ways: from US saving bonds to tax-free municipal bonds, from corporate bonds to money markets and certificates of deposit.

Real estate – Real estate is perhaps the most easily understood and oldest asset class investors. You can make money by investing in real estate in several ways, but it comes down to either owning something and letting others use it for lease payments or rent, or developing property and selling it for profit.

Intangible property and rights – Intangible property consist of everything from patents and trademarks to copyrights and music royalties.

Farmland and other commodity-producing goods – investment in commodity-producing activities involve extracting or producing something from nature or the ground. It usually involves improving it and selling it to make a profit. If there is oil on your land, you can extract it and get cash. If you grow corn, you can sell it and make money. It can involve a lot of risks – disasters, weather, and other challenges that might make you lose money – but you can still make money from it.

2. Decide how you want to own these assets

When you have decided on the assets you want to own, you can decide how you to own them. To understand this point, let's look at business equity. Let's say you want a stake in a publicly traded business. Will you go for shares outright or will you go through a pooled structure?

- **Outright ownership** – This way, you will directly buy shares from an individual company and you will see them in your balance sheet or that of the entity you own. You will be an actual share shareholder and have voting rights. It might give you access to dividend income. Your net worth might rise as the company grows.

- **Pooled ownership** – With this method, you will add your money to a pool contributed to by other people and buy ownership through a shared entity or structure. Most of the time, this is done through mutual funds. If you are a wealthy investor, you can invest in hedge funds. If you don't have a large amount of money, you can consider investing index funds and exchange-traded funds.

3.   Decide where you want to hold the assets

When you have made up your mind on how you want to acquire investment assets, you need to decide how you want to hold these assets. There are several options:

- **Taxable account** – If you decide on taxable accounts like a brokerage account, you will pay tax later but there won't be any restrictions on your money. You will be free to spend it on anything you want. You will be free to cash in and buy anything you want. You can also add any amount you want to it every year.

- **Tax shelters** - If you choose to invest in things like Roth IRA or 401(k) plan, there are tax and asset protection benefits. Some retirement plans and accounts offer unlimited bankruptcy protection. This means that should a medical disaster strike that wipes out your balance sheet, the creditors won't touch your investment capital. Some are tax-deferred. This means you might get tax deductions when you deposit the capital into an account to choose investment and pay taxes in the future. Good tax planning can mean massive extra wealth in the future.

•   **Trust other asset protection mechanisms** – You can hold your investments through structures or entities like trust funds. You will get major asset protection and planning benefits when you use these special ownership methods. This is useful when you want to restrict how your capital is used. Also, if you have significant real estate investments or operating assets, you can speak to your attorney to set up a holding company.

The information you need to start building your personal assets

There are a lot of ways to build personal assets with little money, but few people know how to do it. What could be the problem? The problem is most people don't know about the important process of asset building.

What should one do to build assets? It's not rocket science. If you learn the process of asset building, the rest is easy.

Invest money to accumulate assets

You should know all about the relationship between asset accumulation and investments.

•   **Investments** – Investing is the process of buying assets. Investments are generally made in either stocks, bonds, or cash equivalents. Investments are made with the intention of generating income and earning profits over time. When investments succeed, they are a great way to make passive income. In other words, money gets made without the need for daily upkeep.

- **Asset accumulation** – When you gradually acquire assets over time and hold it for the long term, assets will start to accumulate. These assets consist of your earnings, savings, and the returns on your investments.

- **Asset building** – Asset building is the process of gradually buying assets or acquiring resources with the intention of accumulation. This practice can help families achieve stability, create good credit, save for the future, and ultimately strengthen their communities.

When you buy assets without the intention of accumulation, it becomes a meaningless activity. Without them, it is much more difficult to save for the future.

Since you now understand the process of asset building, let's ask a more basic question.

Why build assets?

If you're interested in achieving financial independence, then you'll want to consider building assets. Why is that necessary?

Do you love your job? I know few people who would raise their hands to that question. If most people don't love their jobs, why do they keep them? It's simple: we need the money so we feel we don't have another choice. It all comes down to the basic need for survival. We think our jobs are inextricably linked to this.

We must compromise to do our jobs because we want to continue earning income. Is there a way to remove this dependency? You may not believe this, but it's absolutely possible. All you have to do is make the necessary changes to your lifestyle and spending habits to achieve financial independence. It's much easier than you think. Here is an approach to help you.

• Realize that you depend on your job for income and understand that there is an alternative. Most people who work don't realize that financial independence exists.

• Start eliminating financial dependence gradually. You can do this by generating an alternative source of income. Where will your alternative source of income come from? From investing in assets. Consider which assets will add the biggest value to your life.

How can a common man build assets?

For those who are already affluent, asset building methods are different. How can a common man build assets? Here are the steps:

1. **Save** – Saving money is very important. The easiest way one can save money is by putting aside some of their income. Eliminating unnecessary spending will increase cash-in-hand. Even millionaires must save money if they want to stay rich. If you save above 25% of your total income, that is considered a decent saving. You can make an automatic transfer where 25% of your money goes automatically to your savings account.

Saving money also allows you to have more money to invest with. When you make larger investments, you can expect bigger returns when the money multiplies.

Here are some other ideas to help you keep more money in your bank account.

• **Build an emergency fund** – Nothing eats assets

faster than an emergency. When something unexpected happens, it can consume a lot of money. An example is a medical emergency. It's recommended that you keep sufficient back-up to handle emergencies. Consider saving for an emergency in cash and insurance.

- **Arrange a recurring deposit** – The priority here is to save. You shouldn't think about a return. There are some advantages to recurring deposits. Savings will be automatic, money is safe, and money remains in the bank.

  Building an emergency fund ensures that we are prepared to meet life's emergencies. When they happen, we can depend on our savings. Arranging for recurring deposits ensures that what we save can be used for investments.

2.   Invest – Why do you need to invest and not keep building savings to buy assets directly? It would be nice to do that, but holding your money as savings isn't recommended. That's because savings can easily be spent. And don't forget, investing your money makes it multiply.

When you have gone through all the effort of saving, you should ensure that you invest that money wisely. Most people have no idea how. Here are some examples of different investments you can make. Many investment experts even advise utilizing more than one method.

- **Hybrid funds** – Hybrid funds have a SIP, which is a useful tool for investments. There are several benefits. You will get exposure to debt and equity from one window. You should develop a mindset to keep you investing in this fund through SIPs. Keep doing this month after month without stopping.

100

- **Index ETFs** – ETFs, also known as Exchange-Traded Funds, can make a worthwhile investment and can encompass many types of investments, such as bonds, stocks, and other types.
  ETFs offers great investment diversification within an equity portfolio. You can get ETF units every time there is above a 3% dip in an index.
- **Gold** – Gold can be a long-term investment that takes up to 12 years. Unlike the other forms of investments, you can actually hold this investment in your own hands.
- **Buy land** – Land is an asset that has become scarce. It's a great idea to invest in land on the outskirts of a city, though all investments in land can be risky. This is because it doesn't produce an income unless you do something with it, and in the meantime, it can cost you a lot in taxes. If you're considering investing in land, make sure you have a plan, and it may be wise to talk to an expert.
- **Trade Cryptocurrencies** – This method of investing is not devoid of its risks, but many people insist there's a lot more money to be made in cryptocurrency investments. In recent years, many bitcoin investors have made fortunes, though many have also lost. Cryptocurrencies can bring you big rewards when invested in wisely. We advise educating yourself before purchasing any.

3. Locked funds – This step is very important. Most people would stop at step two. In this step, you will be converting all your assets into income generating assets. How can this be done? You can consider REITs, rental properties, and dividend-paying stocks.

Since the above steps are very crucial to asset building, let's go into more detail on how we can implement them successfully.

The money you locked in land, SIP, and RD has only one objective. You can redeem it and use it to buy assets at some point. You can use it on income generating assets. Consider the following:

- **Dividend-paying stocks** – These are strong stocks which pay regular dividends to the shareholder. You should buy these stocks at the right price. If you fail to do so, its yield will be too low. You should wait for a perfect time to get the best dividend paying stocks.
- **Rental property** – This might be the best income generating asset you can get, as it generates the best passive income and depending on the property, this passive income can be a sizable sum. What you earn from real estate property also increases the rate of inflation.

You should consider distributing your investments among the above options. These are perfect investment vehicles for income generation.

What's the difference between trading and investing?

Both trading and investing involve making a profit by buying and selling stocks. What sets them apart, however, is how they go about achieving those goals. Trading is more concerned with using the stock market for short-term gains, while investments are usually a long-term commitment that takes place over years and sometimes even decades.

Trading involves higher risks than investing, but also higher returns. This is because stock prices can fluctuate a lot within a short period of time. Timing is, in fact, a major factor that needs to be considered, in the world of trading.

Investing is significantly lower in risk, but don't expect any big returns right away. Investments can get you big rewards, but these will take some time.

How to make successful investments and get big rewards

Now that you're no longer relying on material goods, you likely have more money to spare for your investments. You may even be interested in stocks. Although it may seem simple at first glance, there's a lot more to trading and investing than simply making a purchase and waiting for the dough to roll in. For the most fruitful outcome, you must stay informed on a variety of different factors.

When it comes to buying stocks, it's not enough to just make any investment or trade. In fact, investing in the wrong thing could result in a major loss. To win big from an investment, you need to make calculated efforts in the right direction. You must consider all your options carefully and resist the urge to throw your money at absolutely anything. To ensure that both your trades and investments are successful, keep these useful tips in mind.

1. Don't just fall for the idea

Let's face it, in this day and age, everyone has a good idea. And as for the great ideas out there, chances are that someone has had the same one before. For this reason, you shouldn't throw your money at just any good idea. Take other factors into account. Which company is in charge of this good idea? What is their business plan? There are many reasons why a good idea could lead to a loss or nothing at all. Instead of falling for the idea, fall for the company instead.

2. Always do the research

You may get a good feeling right from the get-go, but good feelings can be wrong. Don't let your financial future suffer for it. Traders should always do their research. Not just into various companies, but also trading patterns and other trends. Resist the urge to wing it and stay completely informed on the entire trading landscape. Understand that everything can affect what happens to your hard-earned money.

3. Spread out your investments

A good tip for avoiding huge losses is to make sure you don't invest in solely one company. Instead, try spreading out your investments between a few different options. Learn from the old saying, "Don't keep all your eggs in one basket." It rings particularly true for investing. This way, if any loss occurs, it won't be catastrophic and you'll still have stocks in other companies. If disaster strikes a company you've invested in, you won't make a huge loss. It may seem unlikely for this to happen, but this is exactly the type of attitude that can lead to losses from carelessness. Many investors have lost billions by failing to take this precaution. For example, in the Enron company scandal.

4. Take some risks

Studies have shown that the crushing disappointment we feel when we lose money is greater than the joy we feel when we win. To avoid these negative feelings, many investors and traders avoid making any risks at all in their pursuits. While we don't advise making big risks all the time, it can pay off to take a leap every now and then. Sometimes you can get very lucky. Just make sure that, should a loss occur, it won't affect your financial standing in a significant way. Make smart risks and you just might find yourself making big returns.

5. Don't overestimate your abilities

After all the time and effort spent staring at the screen, you've finally made a return. Congrats! While this is definitely something to celebrate, don't let your winners' high cloud your judgment. You're not invincible and you could easily lose it all if you don't continue to be careful. Rewards don't always indicate the skill of a trader, sometimes it can all be down to luck. Don't take any wild risks on an impulse. Always invest wisely.

Remember to try and enjoy the world of investing. While it's true that there are many risky aspects to it, it'll bring you more satisfaction and control than putting that same money in needless items. To truly honor the minimalist philosophy, only invest in what you really believe in, and resist the urge to invest in everything.

Greater life satisfaction will come when you take control of your finances back from every whim, fleeting desire and impulse. This is the minimalist way.

Conclusion

Thank you for making it to the end of the Minimalist Budget Mindset.

Let's hope it was informative and able to provide you with all the information you need to manage your money well and achieve your financial goals. With more tools in your money-saving arsenal, you'll find it much easier to take those strides towards financial freedom.

You have learned that minimalism can put an end to the gluttony of the world that surrounds us. It's the opposite of what you see in advertisements on TV. We live in a society that prides itself on buying a lot of needless products; we are overwhelmed by consumerist habits, clutter, material possessions, debt, noise, and distractions. What we don't seem to have enough of, however, is true meaning in our lives and intentionality in our actions. With all you've learned, you'll find it much easier to shut out the noisy consumerist world, with its many money-grabbing ploys.

Adopting a minimalist lifestyle will allow you to eliminate the things you don't need so you can concentrate on what really completes your life. Once you start shifting your values, the money-saving techniques we've demonstrated we'll feel like second nature.

You have learned exactly how you can save money as a minimalist. Saving money this way has a lot of benefits and it could save you a lot of distress in the future. You have learned how to track your spending and how you can start saving money. This has taught you how to be disciplined when money is involved.

Other than that, you have learned some of the best budgeting strategies to help you achieve your goals. Apply these strategies as soon as you can to achieve financial goals sooner than you expect. Don't feel daunted, as you may find them easier than you think.

Getting out of debt has never been easy for most of us, but learning about the causes of debt has helped you view debt differently and learn effective ways to get out of it. These methods will help you get out of debt while at the same time helping you save more.

When you have eliminated debt and learned how to save, consider investing in something that will multiply your money. With the information you have learned about investing, and the life-altering self-discipline you have gained, you will view investing from a different angle and start accumulating personal wealth. Use your newly discovered tips wisely to ensure you minimize any potential losses and make more frequent gains.

You've now learned how to develop a minimalist mindset and make the big savings that all successful minimalists do. Practice makes perfect, and that's what you need to do with your new minimalist budget mindset. With some time and practice, you will be able to make use of good money habits and make it your part of life.

Lastly, if you enjoyed this book I ask that you please take the time to review it on Audible.com. Your honest feedback would be greatly appreciated.

Thank you.